I would like to dedicate this book to my little brother, Herman Eleton Mccray Jr. Brother I love you so very much. Thank you for every conversation and all the love you have shown me. In dedication of your life this is my gift to you. You are forever loved and never will be forgotten. I promised you I would write a book for you and here it is. I hope you love it. I love you forever..... Yours Truly~Big Sis~

*I would also like to dedicate this book to my only son, Wisdom Junya Prophecy Kizer. Mommy loves you very much. Thank you for choosing me to be your mother. I promise to protect and love you like no other. You name and soul carries a huge part of my heart. Life is not easy, but I promise to show you how to navigate through it. Here is a gift to you, so you may have long after I leave this Earth... Mommy loves you always and forever!!
Yours Truly~Mommy~*

TABLE OF CONTENTS

Chapter 1: What are you doing, Junya?

Chapter 2: Don't worry big sis! I'm coming right back!

Chapter 3: Breathe Bro! You Promised!

Chapter 4: Visions

Chapter 5: The Bigger Picture

Chapter 6: Junya's Last Performance

Chapter 7: Forgive those that trespass against you!

Chapter 8: What if?

Chapter 9: Wisdom Junya Prophecy

Chapter 10: FEAR... False Evidence Appearing Real

Chapter 1: What are you doing, Junya?

    2020 has shown me so much! I learned that I am a lightworker, put on here Earth to bring peace and unity to the world. One of my gifts is writing to you. Another gift of mine is my voice to do the same exact thing. Since a child I was able to do this, but the year 2020 has shown me everything clearly. Many of the answers that I needed, have been answered by the universe to me. One story that has been placed inside of me is about one of my brothers. This one is my younger brother. He is two years younger than me, but acts like he is the oldest.

    My little brother's name is Herman Eleton Mccray Jr. Everyone calls him, Junya or Herm Junya. I simply call him baby bro! I remember one year speaking with him about him becoming a rapper and making a clothing line. He was extremely excited about this dream. I gave him advice and stood back and watched him achieve this dream. As I watch him grow, I saw a lot of envy and jealousy from some of his associates grow with him. It started to get worst and I felt I needed to step in and have a serious conversation with him. I remember reaching out and listening about all that was going on to see how I could help the situation. He spoke about certain people that he knew that did not like him or the attention he was receiving. He also spoke about wanting to leave South Carolina because his dreams were bigger than he could imagine. I was so proud of him and told him that moving to New York would be perfect for him, because a lot more people here shared large dreams as well, and it would not be as much jealousy then in a small town. He told me he wanted to visit to see how everything was, but he was on probation because of a charge he received, and he would not, at the time be able to leave that state. I was upset with him, but I understood. I told him to finish probation and stay out of trouble so we could make the trip happen and he could see something different then what he saw down there. We would always tell each other that we love one another before we hung up the phone. After that I continued to keep an eye on him because I was always worried. I continued to check in with him through phone calls and video chat to make sure he was doing everything he needed to do. My baby brother Junya!

One day when I woke up and went on Facebook, I saw a post from a group of people I was friends with talking about my little brother. When I clicked the post, the conversations were hard to read knowing they were talking about my little brother. I saw horrible photos of him bruised as if he was in a fight. The people were laughing and sharing the photos everywhere. I knew they did not know that was my brother that they were talking about, but that did not stop the anger I felt. I immediately reached out to Junya to see what was going on and if he was okay. I called him on the phone and quickly hung up, because I needed to see his face while I spoke to him, so I called him on video chat instead. When he answered, it took everything in me not to shed a tear. I was so angry and upset. I asked him what happened, and he told me he was jumped and robbed. He told me it was nothing to him and the guys was just jealous of him. He said he do not want to get in anymore trouble that would set him back. He spoke about some new plans he had for expansion and that made me incredibly happy and enormously proud of him to be able to still see light through the darkness he was experiencing. I explained how proud of him I was and that he better hurry and come to New York, because I hated him down there going through what he was going through.

He was always so strong though and told me that he was good. I told him that I would go live on Facebook to address how I feel about the situation and tell them to back off him. He said leave it alone, but I said it was only right I stepped in as his big sister and because the people that I saw it from, were some of my Facebook friends. He told me how much he loved and appreciate me, and I said to him the same. We made an agreement that he would check in with me every week and not to get into any more problem that would prevent our plan from succeeded. After that phone call ended, I jumped on Facebook to address the issue and to tell people to leave my little brother alone. I said how I felt about the situation and left it as that. I had a lot of support under the post from my friends and family and his as well. I still worried a lot about him though.

A couple of days before Thanksgiving in 2016 my family and I went to visit South Carolina for the first time since we moved to New York in 2003. We had an amazing time. I was able to see some of my siblings from my father's side that lived in South Carolina. I called Junya and he brought my younger sisters to see me. My oldest brother came as well. We had a great time. My mother's side of my family was able to meet some of my sisters and brother from my father's side. It was amazing to see us all there and connecting as if we all knew each other forever. I loved it. I remember pulling my little brother to the side and telling him I wanted to buy some of his clothes. He told me he had none with him and he would have to send it to me in New York. He saw the sad look on my face, so he asked what size I wore and took off the sweater he had on and gave it to me. I was still upset because I wanted more, but to know he took the shirt off his back to make me happy was even better. That was him. He always wanted people around him happy. I love him so much! I love them all so much. We all continued to enjoy each other's company for the rest of the night.

A few months later in 2017 when I checked on Facebook, I noticed he had a video that went viral. I was so happy until I clicked on it and saw Junya punching this guy. I was so angry with him. What the hell was all our conversations about I thought. I called him and at first, he did not answer, so I called him again and he answered. He said, "I know why you are calling big sis, let him explain." He said that the guy he hit was the same guy that robbed him, and made a song dissing him and his new music. Junya said the guy knew he was in the club when he started performing the dissing track and that made Junya angry. So, he punched him, and someone was recording it and posted it on Facebook, and it went viral. I said, "that story did not make me feel any better." I told him that it would only bring more problems and he should stop sharing it. I said, "people carry grudges for long periods of time and even though they did wrong things to you, they do not think you should do wrong things to them." I told him that by the video going viral the guy would only become full of hate, envy, and revenge. I begged him to leave it alone. Then I told him that he needed to leave South Carolina again. He told me he had nine more months on probation then he could leave. He said he would leave it alone and I told him I would be watching him. He did not leave it alone right then, but he eventually did.

I was so happy when all the confusion died down and I saw him focusing on music and his clothing line. It was great for him and a lot of people loved and supported him. He is a great guy and never selfish. He always brought others into his videos, and he would have events for the children while they wore his clothing line. That was the little brother I knew and was waiting for him to shine. I was so proud he was doing his thing. I continue to watch him and post him on my page. We would speak a lot and he would keep me posted about how everyone was doing. On my birthday, January 19, 2018, I posted me wearing the sweater he gave me. I loved that sweater so much. His clothing was made perfect! No matter how much I wore or washed the sweater his name never messed up or peel off. The gold and the material he used was like nothing I have ever seen before, and I told him that. I was so proud of him because that clothing line was a brilliant idea. I never met anyone like him before. He completely believed in everything he touched. Everything he saw was not only a vision, but he also brought it to life. Once he made his brand, he wore everything with his name on it. His clothing, his socks, his jewelry, and his tattoos. I loved it. My little brother was shining like the star he is. No one could take that away from him even if they did not believe in him, he believed in himself. He inspires me so much to continue my dreams and not just work for somebody else in this lifetime. He told me that if I did not believe in myself then no one would believe in me. He told me that independence was in our blood and that I should find out what makes me happy and go for it. He always gave the best advice and sounded like an older brother instead of a younger one. I thanked him for the advice, and he told me that he was just giving me what I always gave him.

At the end of year 2018 I saw a post of my brother with a woman and she was pregnant. Her and my brother was at what it seemed to be their baby shower. I was so happy I was going to be an auntie. Then shortly after, I saw on my brother's Facebook page what seemed to be him with another girl at a baby shower that seemed to be his as well. I was confused so I called him. As usual, he knew why I was calling. He explained the situation to me, basically saying he had gotten two females pregnant around the same time and their due dates were close. I told him I was extremely angry with him, because he was cheating on females and he had sisters and a mother. I also explain that it would be difficult to manage two baby mothers and keep them both happy. Then I explained to him that our plan of him coming to live in New York would also be difficult when he was supposed to just stay out of trouble and not make things more complicated. I told him that I was proud of him for finishing probation though and asked him how he would manage the situation that he had in front of him. He told me that he was just going to be honest with both woman and support them through the trouble that was caused. He said no matter what, he promised me that he would be the best father that he could be to both children. I believed him because I knew he loved kids and I also knew he was a loving person. I told him I love him, and I will be watching and keeping in contact to make sure he was doing what he had to. After that conversation I knew that it would be almost impossible to get him away from South Carolina, but if he was not getting into all that other trouble, I was okay with it.

Chapter 2: Do not worry big sis! I am coming right back!

I continued to keep in contact with Junya and support him as much as I could. He ended up having a little boy that was born on February 9, 2019 and a little girl born on February 14, 2019. Everything was okay until a little while after the babies were born a lot of conflict arise for him. When I would speak to him, he would be sad, because one woman would not let him see the baby out of jealousy he would say. I told him that he had to figure something out to make them both happy, and it would only get worst. It did get worst. It was all over Facebook and the law got involved. It resulted in the woman hating each other, and Junya not seeing one of his babies. It was horrible and he was hurt. It was a messy situation, and we would always talk about it. I prayed for him a lot. I prayed for the children and peace. I also prayed for the mothers of the children.

In December of 2019, my mother, two younger sisters, and my oldest sister was planning a trip to South Carolina. Junya wanted me to come, but I just had my third baby girl two months before in October and was not up for leaving her so soon. I told him that my mom and sisters were going, and I wanted him to make sure they were good while being down there. He promised, so I knew he would do just that. At that time, I also was working on a book I wanted to publish that meant a lot to me. I also had been working on myself and did not want to party or be around drinking or nothing like that. They really enjoyed their selves though. Junya called me with details, then I spoke to my younger sister shortly after with their details of the time they had. One thing Junya told me was that they did not have to want for anything, and he think he fell in love with my little sister. My little sister name is Jamerella, but we call her Rella. At the time I did not believe him, because he always told me how pretty she is and he would love to date her, but she never gave him the time of the day.

When I spoke to my younger sister, she confirmed what Junya had told me earlier that day. They told me that my brother is a gentleman and he made sure they had an amazing time. That made me smile to hear the stories of how he was with them. They all seemed incredibly happy. Then my younger sister told me that she liked my little brother and she think she would like to see where things go with them. At that moment, I had mixed feeling because I never really thought they would connect or anything. I did not really state how I felt I just thought I would wait it out. I knew Junya had problems with two females down there and my younger sister had problems with a guy she was dating for years. I had mixed feelings because I prayed for Junya's happiness all the time and I prayed that someone came and swept my younger sister off her feet and showed her just how a woman should be treated. At the time I guess I could not see how this would work out because of all the drama.

About three weeks later they made it official. Junya called and spoke to me about it and asked how I felt. I told him I did not know how to feel about the situation and if it is going to continue, he had to get the woman in line, and he could not hurt my sister. I spoke to my younger sister and told her that she would have to get that guy she was dating away from her and she could not hurt my brother. It felt so weird to me at the route they were going, but the love that I felt surrounding them both, it was nothing I could do but support them.

Junya called me a week before New Years of 2020 and said, he was finally coming to New York. I told him I would believe it when I saw it. After I got off the phone I kind of knew he was being honest, because he was in love and that was the only thing that would really make him up and leave down south. On December 27, 2019 I surrendered my life to God. I forgave myself for everything that I have done in the past and I forgave everyone for anything that I felt was done to me. I was in an incredibly good space with myself and the energy around me. Two days later, I published my first book and was extremely proud of myself. That book meant a lot to me and publishing it tell my story meant even more. I remember Junya called me the next day telling me how proud of me he was and telling me that he booked his ticket and was really coming to New York. Everything seemed so perfect. My book was selling like crazy and I received a lot of feedback. My family was happy, and the ball was soon to drop in one day. I just knew that 2020 would be an amazing year.

Junya arrived in New York on December 31, 2020 that was is my second daughter's 6th birthday. He went to my younger sister house to spend some time with her first, which I understood. They were in love and

I respected it. He was only going to be up here for a couple of days, and I wanted him to myself when we spend time. I was a little upset, but it was just a feeling because I got over it two days later when I picked him up from her house.

      He looked like an angel walking into my arms. When I hugged him all the memories we shared came in a blink of an eye. I started crying because it felt so good to finally see him keep his promise to come to New York even if it was only for a couple of days. When I looked at him, he looked so happier than I have been seeing him from the drama that was occurring down south. Then we entered my jeep and started on our journey. We talked about everything on the way back to my house. We spoke about how he felt being in New York. He told me he loved it and he felt like it was home for him, because he felt free here. He said that my younger sister took him to a couple of places to get some insight. He was in love with my little sister and they were talking about him moving up here for good. Then I asked him how that would work with his children's mothers. He had a whole plan of how he would travel back and forth to see his children, and if their mothers allowed him, he would bring them to New York sometimes. We spoke about clothing connections and music connections in New York as well.

    I remember looking at him every time he spoke about my little sister and saw his face light up with a glow I never seen before. So, I asked him if he was serious about her. He looked at me with a real serious face and said he loved her so much. He told me that she made him feel like the best man in the world. He said he never got that feeling from a woman. She is naturally beautiful, independent, intelligent, a great mother, she can cook, and a great motivator and supporter for him. When he looked at me and described her that way, I told him that he was right and if he hurt her then he would have to answer to me. He told me that he was so serious about her and right after he attended his kids party he is coming back to New York and ask her to marry him. My younger sister birthday is on February 19, so that meant he was coming right back. I look at him and said, "I felt some type of way because you are my younger brother, and she is my younger sister. It took this to happen for you to bring your butt to New York but looking at you both and the way you guys feel about one another, reminded me of a prayer I prayed." Then I asked Junya how did all this happened? He said he had no clue. I said, "I do, because I prayed for you both to be happy, but I never thought it would be together. I guess you have to be careful what you pray for huh"! We both laughed.

    While I was looking for parking, Junya said that he wanted to go to the store and buy my second daughter a gift for her birthday. So instead of parking at my house, we went around the corner to the shopping area. Junya was paranoid about everything. He kept looking around as if we were being followed and I would ask what he was looking for. He asked me if the police bothered me a lot up here or stopped me. I told him that you must really be doing something crazy to get stopped like not following the traffic rules. Other than that, the police did not really stop you. I told him I was only stopped twice since I was driving, and both times were my fault. He told me you do not even have to be doing anything down south and the police would just bother you. He said on top of watching for the cops he had to watch out for people that did not like him. I asked what he meant because the way I saw it everyone loved him. He told me that just because people seemed to like him, does not mean they really supported him. "No matter what you do for people they could always be plotting against you", he said. He told me that a lot of fights and drama he had was from people that once was his friends or people close to him that seemed like they liked him. I listened to him in shock. A lot of things we spoke about started to make sense of some of the things that he was going through. I told him that is why he needed to be in New York where no one knew him, and he could kind of start over and have less hate. He agreed.

  We parked the car and I asked him what he wanted to get her. He said he wanted to get her some sneakers, so we walked to Footlocker. When we got in Footlocker, we debated about what sneakers to get her then he saw the perfect ones. They were the hot pink, orange, white, and silver #12 Jordan that just dropped. He said they would be perfect for the spring season. He also said we should get her a bigger size so she could wear them by Easter. I agreed, then he paid for them and we left the store and headed for the car. Before we reached the car, we passed by this store with lots of suits in them and these shiny shoes that caught Junya's eyes. He said, "Big sis those are fire"! When I looked at them, I agreed. I knew my brother loved shiny shoes a lot and those were shiny. He wanted to go try them on, so we entered the store and he asked for his size. When he tried both shoes on, he started jumping saying that people down south are going to be mad when he enters the club. He did the George Jefferson walk and I just stood to the side of him and admired his confidence. We had so much in common. I loved shiny things too. So, I thought they were hot. Then he said he was going to need some black pants to go with them. He picked out some black pants and tried them on and bought both. The owner was trying to sell him some other shoes that he also liked, and he told them not to worry he would be back to their store every time he came back to New York. I could see him going back to that store every time he came back because they had all his styles that he liked in there. When we walked out of the store, I asked him if he was hungry and he said he wanted me to take him to a place that had the best baked macaroni and cheese. I told him I knew the perfect spot, but it was fifteen minutes away from where we were.

When we arrived at the place where the best macaroni and cheese was, he said he was starving. The place I took him to is considered a Jamaican restaurant. One of the best I knew. I told him it was Jamaican food, so the macaroni and cheese may not taste the way us southern folks make it. He said he did not care he would try it. We proceeded to order. He ordered baked macaroni and cheese, Jerk wings, and rice and peas. Then he told me to get whatever I wanted, and he would pay. He always was that way. A gentleman that also reminded me of a big brother. I ordered just Jerk wings. We sat and ate there. We found a seat at the window where we could see outside the restaurant. We ate and talked. He said the macaroni and cheese was okay, but their food was not better than my little sister. He complimented her food so highly. While he complimented her, I looked at him in his eyes and saw how much he really loved her. I told him he sounded like he really was in love and he looked at me and with this serious face said, "Big sis she is everything to me"! I was so happy he was happy and happy I could look him in his eyes because he was right in my face.

We finish eating and went to my house so he could spend some time with his three nieces before he left us. On our way back on the highway I told him that I signed a lease at a new place and pointed to the new place as we passed it. I told him that by the time he came back to New York I would be already moved into the new apartment. He told me that I better take him there and I said of course I would and there would always be a spot for him in my home. We arrived at the corner of my house and he said he wanted to go to the liquor store to grab some Hennessy. I told him I did not drink anymore, and I really did not like it in my house, but because it was him, I would allow it just this once. He got the liquor, and we went up the street to my house. When we got there, he was so happy to see all three of his nieces. I put the drink in the kitchen on top of the fridge while he gave them hugs. He met my oldest daughter and middle daughter when we went to South Carolina a few years prior, so they remembered him, but he never met the baby I just had two months before his visit. He hugged my oldest daughter first her name is D'ziyah. She was just smiling while he told her how big she was and how she looked just like our younger sister. Then he hugged my middle daughter telling her Happy Birthday. Her name is Heaven. She started smiling while he gave her the shoes, he bought her earlier. She opened the box and started smiling even harder. She said, "Wow! Thank you, uncle Junya! I love them. They are beautiful." He was happy she loved them, and I was happy to see him with them. My newborn was asleep. Her name is Royal. I let her rest a little longer while he rekindled with the two oldest. They talked and joked with each other on one couch while I watched from the other couch. While they were talking, he looked up at me and asked why I was looking at him the way I was and I said, "I'm simply happy you are here. I love you and miss you so much."

After they finish laughing and joking me and him stepped into the kitchen. I made ice for his drink and we talked. We talked about life and our goals. We talked about plans that we could do with each other. He gave me some good connections and ideas for my business. I told him the breakdown of the next books I wanted to publish. He said, "Look at us big sis! This is what I am missing down south. I could talk to you about so much. I feel at home and at ease up here. I do not have to constantly watch my back every second. I really like it here." We talked about how he was going to travel back and forth from South Carolina to New York and make everything work out for the best. I told him I felt the same way about him being around me. I could speak to him about what I was feeling and my crazy ideas and not actually feel crazy. He told me that none of my dreams were crazy and impossible. He told me no matter how big they are and crazy they may sound when you tell others, always follow them. People could not see his visions until they came to the light. Then they understood. He said, "Look at me! I made a song about Captain Planet and wore the suit when I opened for Lil' Boosie (A known rapper around the world)."

We laughed at it and he said it was not until he did it that people understood his vision. He told me how he started from nothing and eventually worked his way up unto having his own brand that was incorporated and his own clothing line that no one could take from him. He said at first no one believed in him or his vision, but they had to respect it when he wore everything with his name on it. He said, "You must believe in yourself more than anyone else." "Not only do I wear my brand on all my clothes, but I also even have my chain named after it and a tattoo so it would never leave me even if I die." Looking at him saying all those things made my ideas pour even more into my head and it gave me some type of empowerment. I said, 'Look at you teach your big sister like you are the big one!"

He drunk his Hennessy while we continued to talk, then my youngest daughter started crying. I went to grab her from her crib while he said he was going to wash his hand so he could hold her. When I got back to the living room with her, he was talking to D'ziyah and looked at me smiling. I gave him the receiving blanket to put over his clothes and place Royal in his hands. He held her as if he were a pro at holding babies. She did not cry at all she just looked at him. Then I made her a bottle while he sat on the couch and talk to her. He said she looked just like his son when he was born. He said our genes are extremely strong. I agreed with him as I handed him the bottle to feed her. Royal was in his hands, Heaven was on his right side, and D'ziyah was on his left side. I was on the sofa across from them staring at him. I was so excited to see him in my living room with his nieces. I kept staring at them, then I took some photos of them just the way they were sitting. He asked me to take a photo with him. I said, "Not this time Junya, I'm not prepared. When you come back next month, then we could have our photo time." He really wanted that photo, but he let it go because he knew how women are with their photos. I took more photos of him, and Royal fell asleep in his arms. I asked D'ziyah to put her back into her bed while me and Junya talked some more. Junya wanted to smoke, so I took him into the hallway stairwell so he could.

When we got into the hallway, he asked me where my fiancé was because he wanted to meet him. I told him that he was taking care of his grandmother and he would meet him when he returned. Then he started getting into father mode. He asked me how he was treating me and was I happy with him. I answered his questions while laughing. He told me that he always worries about me the same way I am with him, even though he knows I could handle myself. Then he said the way I speak about my dreams and the way I write my books he could picture me on Oprah's talk show. I told him I appreciate that, and it was funny he said that because my fiancé told me the exact same thing. He told me to start writing to different talk shows about my book. He also said to write radio shows as well to help get the word out for my book. He told me someone that made a famous sauce down south did that and now their sauce is talked about everywhere. I listened and wrote notes on all the things he told me to do.

"He is so smart and talented," I thought to myself. I thanked him for all the advice and asked him if he would like another drink. He said, "yes," so I poured him another drink. We went back into the living room and relax with the children. He started telling D'ziyah all the great things he heard about her and when he returned, he would take her to the basketball court and show her some new moves for the season. She told him that they were undefeated, and she might show him some new moves. We laughed and continued to talk until it got dark outside. Then Rella called him asking me and him to come pick her up from her son's grandparents' house. I agreed and told my babysitter to watch the children as we left. He hugged them all and gave them kisses. Heaven asked him when he was coming back, and he told her the following month. She was happy and said, "Okay", with a huge smile. She told him she loved him.

The babysitter arrived and we left. We got into the car and started going towards our destination. Junya had me play this song he liked. I played it twice for him then I told him that I wanted him to listen to this song I liked. He really liked that song I played and kept wanting to hear it. He asked me about the song. He asked who made the song. When did the song came out because he never heard it before? I answered all his questions. While we were talking, my sister called him asking him how far we were. He looked at me and asked me the same question and I told him that we were fifteen minutes from her. He told her and hung up the phone. He started sweating a little and looking worried. I told him that I would rush because I knew how impatient my little sister was.

He looked relieved and told me that he never wants her to be upset with him. He said also that she had my nephew with her, and he would get a chance to meet him. He said they spoke a lot on the phone and facetime, but never face to face. I told him not to worry because he was a great kid and you are great with kids, so he is going to love you. I was so happy that he felt the way he felt. I could tell he was perfect for my little sister. He cared about how she felt, cared about what she thought, wanted to make her happy, and spoke very highly of her as if she was his queen. She really needed someone like that, and he really needed someone to treat him and care for him the way she did as well.

We got to where Rella was waiting, and they entered the car. She was with her best friend, and her son. She introduced my brother to her son and her best friend. He asked if she wanted to sit in the front seat and she said no. She told me and him we could spend the rest of the ride together because he was going to stay with her for the night. I was happy because I felt the same way. I turned the music up and continue driving and singing my favorite song. After my favorite song went off, I just let the playlist play. That ride felt great because I had my little brother on the passenger side of me and he was happy.

When we arrived at Rella's house, I helped them out of the back seat, and gave my nephew a big hug and told him I love him. Then I said goodnight to my little sister and her best friend. Me and Junya went to open the trunk to get their bags and we looked at each other and gave each other a huge hug. It was so tight that you could hear our coats sounding like they slapped each other. I started crying and tried my hardest not to let him see. Of course, he saw me and asked why I was crying. I said, "I just love you so much and miss you!" He said the same thing and told me not to worry, because we had a lot of time to spend together.

My little sister got impatient and started to walk across the street. I did not care though because I knew I would not get to see him until he came back. Apart of me started to feel as if I would never see him in New York again. I shook that feeling off though. I told him I would walk with him across the street to make sure he is safe. He laughed and said, "Why cause you my big sis?" Even though that may have been one reason, my real reasoning for doing that was to receive another hug. When we reached across the street, I hugged him even tighter, and he knew I wanted that hug because he hugged me the same way. Our coats slapped one another again and I just held him a little longer this time because I needed him and a hug. The tears would not stop falling from my eyes. They were falling super-fast this time. I could not stop it. I did not want to. I wanted to get that feeling I felt, to go away. He looked at me and said, "Don't worry big sis! I am coming right back! I promise." I looked at him and told him he better or I would beat him up. I told him to please be careful and that I loved him very much. He told me he loved me too. Then that was enough to clear up how I felt. I just kept telling myself he was coming right back. The more I said it the more I felt better leaving. I got into my car and watch him disappear into her building and I drove home. I was so happy. I was so proud. Everything felt great. We made plans, spend time with each other, and I knew he would eventually want to stay in New York. At least I would have a brother that lived close to me. Everything else would work itself out later.

 The next day I followed him on Snapchat and Facebook social media to make sure he got home safe. I called him and he confirmed he was home. I was happy and I thanked him for coming and told him to kiss his babies for me and I loved him very much. He then told me that Rella was going to South Carolina around my birthday which is January 19th. He asked if I wanted to come and that he would pay for me. I told him I would think about it, but right then and there I said to myself that it was still kind of early to travel and I did not think I was going to go. Plus, I wanted them to spend more time with one another to see if their relationship was serious. He said if I changed my mind (as if he knew I was not going), then just call him and let him know.

Chapter 3: Breathe Bro! You Promised!

Around January 7, 2020 I called Rella for something and while we were talking, she told me that Junya was very unhappy when he went back to South Carolina. I asked her what she meant by that comment. She said that he was depressed about being down there for some reason. She said he no longer felt at home and was starting to become paranoid a little. I asked her why she did not tell him to come back. She said she did, but Junya would not listen. He said he had to make sure everything was perfect for his children's party, so he had to go to work. Then she said he was calling her own Facebook messenger, so she would merge me in. I said okay and hung up the phone and waited for the call.

The call came instantly. I said, "Hey Bro!" He said, "What's up big sis"! I said, "How is it going down there?" He said, "Man sis ever since I landed in South Carolina it felt like a cloud of depression hit me for some reason. I do not feel at home anymore. I feel like I just left home from being with you guys. The love that I got there was different. I did not have to be paranoid about these dam cops. I know there is people who do not like me here. I'm tired of looking over my shoulders man." Right then and there I instantly got depressed for him, because I remembered how he was acting when he was driving with me. He was paranoid about the cops stopping us for everything unto the point where I had to tell him to calm down. I guess I really did not understand how he truly felt because I was not experiencing it. I told him to just drop everything and come back to New York and we will figure everything out from there. He said, "I want to, but I have to work so I could make sure my babies enjoyed their first birthday. Plus, if I miss their first birthday, then I would never be able to see my children because of their mothers. I already must have two separate birthday parties because they do not get along. So, imagine if I miss the party. Don't worry after their party I am going to have a talk with both of their mothers about moving to New York, so we can make arrangements." I could not believe he was considering moving to New York. I asked him if he was sure. He said, "Yes big sis man, I will just fly back and forth until they allow them to come spend the summer in New York with me."

I told him that I understood what he was saying, and I totally agree with him about the children, but as his big sis I must be honest with him and give my opinion. I told him that I think this was an extremely hard situation to be in and I wish he would have been left South Carolina for a while. I said that it is no going back to that so my opinion to him now is to sit down and talk to both mothers at this moment and explain to them how he is feeling. Maybe they would understand. I told him that if he feels he would get in trouble with people that do not like him or the police then I highly suggest he leave. I told him that I learned that our intuition is everything to us and God speaks to us through spirit which communicates to our intuition. I told him I know how he is for his children and I respected him as a father for that, because I am the same way as a mother. If something happens to you before the party, then you would not make it anyways. I told him he could not allow females emotions to make decisions for the safety of his life when you feel highly about what you are feeling. I know you are worried about your children, but they are too young to understand what you are feeling. They would be happier that you are okay versus you being in danger and they cannot see you. I knew he was listening, but I also knew my little brother. Those kids' birthday and happiness meant everything to him, so he had to be there. I told him that I knew he was not going to miss their birthdays because of how he felt, so he had to promise me that he would be safe, stay out the spotlight, give those kids the best party ever and stay away from police. I told him that he could do it that way and then after their birthdays instead of having a sit down with the mothers of his kids he could fly to New York and tell them over the phone, and I would help him. That way he would feel safe, the kids would be happy, and the mothers would respect him for the party he showed up and showed out for. He said that plan was perfect!

I started to get emotional and cried a little silently telling him he had to promise that he would come back to me in one peace. That he would walk away from trouble. He said, "I promise big sis and I love you so much for all the talks and for you always caring about me." I told him it is because I love him! I love all my sisters and brothers. At that moment Rella said, "Love you too Nene"! I totally forgot she was on the phone for a second, but when she spoke, I was incredibly happy that moment of my love could be shared with them both at the same time. I laughed and told Rella to hurry and go down there with him to take his mind off all that nonsense, because he was driving me crazy! She asked me if I was going to go with her. I told her, "No" I think it needs to be just you and him this time. I will go next time. We all laughed, and I told them to continue to talk, because I had some errands to run. We all said I love you and I hung up.

My birthday came shortly after on January 19, 2020. I was so excited! I was exactly where I wanted to be in life. I was with all three of my girls and Fiancé, I just published my first book, I did not have to work because of maternity leave, and my sister was with my brother in South Carolina. Everyone was happy and I was happy. So much love surrounded me. I got so much love from my friends and family on Facebook. So many calls from my friends and family. It was perfect.

It was my 30th birthday! I have been talking to God internally since I surrendered my life on December 29, 2019 and I kept hearing a voice inside telling me to go to church. At that time, I was not really going to church, so I had no church home. I remembered a coworker that I grew to love as a friend named Liliane once told me that she attended a church around the corner from my house. I text her about 7 a.m. that morning to get the address so me and my children could attend. She sent me the address and told me that church did not start until 12 p.m. that evening. I knew my youngest aunt that recently moved to New

York wanted to also attend a church, so I called her and told her if she would be ready, I would pick her up so she could also attend. She agreed and her and her four children got ready and I picked them up and drove to church. When we arrived there and walked inside, we were a bit nervous after not attending church in a while, but that all stopped when I saw Liliane on stage. She smiled at me and I smiled at her and we took a seat in the third row from the front. The ceremony started and her husband was the pastor. I was so shocked. We always spoke about the church she attended, but I never knew that her and her husband owned it. I was simply happy to be there. It felt like it could become my home church.

They preached and I close my eyes to communicate with God as I would always do alone. I felt tears running down my face from any emotions that I had from my life before that day. I was able to let everything go fully. I felt so free. That voice inside spoke to me again and said, "Buy your suit". I opened my eyes and cried even harder, because I thought the message meant that I was going to do something extremely big and important for my future. I felt so much joy. When I turned around and looked at my aunt her face looked as though she needed to be there as well.

The preacher asked us to stand and introduce ourselves. As we did Liliane called me to the front of the church and introduced me to the entire church. She told them who I was and where she met me. She also told them that she was proud of me, because I had just recently published my first book. Then I told her that it was also my birthday that day. She repeated my birthday to the church and ask them to help her show us how they celebrated a birthday. They all stood up and grabbed a chair for me to sit in. Then they all walked to me singing Happy Birthday giving me big hugs and lots of money. I was so shocked. I never experienced anything like that before. My aunt had the same shocked face as I did. She was crying and I was crying while hugging them all back. It was amazing! My daughters were also able to experience that feeling with me which made the day even better. It felt like the best birthday I have ever had. After they sung and given me my gifts, Liliane gave me the microphone to speak. I thanked them all for everything while tears fell from my eyes. I told them how much I appreciate them and love them for having us with open arms. I felt as if I belong with them and could make that church my second home. What an amazing birthday so far and it was still early in the day.

After church we all hugged outside and said our goodbyes to one another. Me, my aunt, and our children walked home in surprise still trying to register what just happened at the church. We talked about it in disbelief over and over. We went back to my house so I could fix us all Sunday dinner. While I was cooking, I received a facetime call from Rella telling me Happy Birthday and then she turned the phone towards Junya. I was so happy to see the glow on their faces. They looked so happy. They looked like they were madly in love and it lit my entire heart up. I told them what I saw in their faces and they both laughed and confirmed just how happy they were.

Junya screamed Happy Birthday to me and told me how proud of me he was. I was so happy to hear that from him. It felt like my father telling me that. He asked me what I wanted for my birthday and to send him my $Cashapp name (an app that allows you to send money back and forth to people for a low price instantly). I told him that I had everything I needed and just wanted our plan to go as plan, so I could see him in a couple of weeks. He promised that he was staying out the way and my little sister said she was staying with him an extra week to make sure he stayed out of trouble. I told him that was all I wanted. I went over some of the things that happened to me in church with him and even he was surprised. He told me I was special, and everyone loved me no matter where I went, I had that effect on people. I just smiled and told him thank you while blushing. He kept asking me to send my $Cashapp name. I told him that he was going to need all his money, because my little sister that I know so well is not cheap. We all laughed, and I told them to have enough fun for me too. We all said we love each other and hung up the phone. That was the last time I spoke to my brother on the phone.

On Sunday February 2, 2020 during church, I heard that voice inside telling me to buy my suits again. So, after church I went into a nearby Burlington to grab me a suit. I found the perfect one and tried it on. When I was about to go pay for them, I thought to myself how I should save money and I did not really need the suits at that moment. I told myself I would come back later to treat myself with it. I always did that when it came down to buying myself something. I guess I am always thinking about my children and them always needing something. So, I would struggle when it was time to treat myself. I ended up not getting the suits at that very moment and just went home. I did feel good about trying it on, so I knew where I was going to purchase it when I needed it.

On February 5, 2020 at around 4:30 p.m. I was on the phone with Thomesha (my second youngest sister from my mother's side). She just picked up Rella from her house to take her to fix her phone that just black out about two hours before. Me and Thomesha was talking about her younger sister on her father's side (We had different fathers). She was telling me some problems that occurred between the two of them. I listened to her and then gave my advice on the situation. I told Thomesha that she must forgive her sister because she was pregnant and going through a lot. I told her that no matter what she is still your younger sister, and they would eventually talk things out. She just needs to be forgiven right now. You must be the strong one no matter what. I told her that I know the words that was exchanged was difficult to carry, but you must forgive quickly. Anything could happen to her and you would never forgive yourself for not being there for her.

She was not really trying to hear me though, but she still listened. Then I could hear Rella getting angry in the background about something. I asked Thomesha what was wrong with her. She told me her phone blacked out and she was rushing to get it fixed. Right then and there I remembered thinking that she just wanted to talk to my brother Junya, because they were always on the phone. After I thought about it Thomesha said it out loud. Then Rella said, "No! I mean that too, but my phone was out for a while and I can't talk to anyone." She sounded so angry and Thomesha was laughing and said, "Yea right she just wants to speak with Junya." I knew, she knew it, and Rella knew it. I told Thomesha to go ahead and get Rella to the store quick and call her younger sister to talk and remember what I said, then call me back to tell me what she said. She agreed and we hung up. I looked at the time, because I was waiting for my fiancé to come back from the store so I could get a simple dinner started. It was about 4:40 p.m. I called my fiancé and he said he was on his way back from the store then we hung up.

Then Thomesha called me back at 4:46 p.m. When I looked at the phone, I remembered thinking it was too soon for her to be calling me back. I knew she did not call her sister that quick. Then I thought maybe she pocket dialed me, so I did not answer. The phone rang again, and it was her, so I knew she was calling me. I answered the phone and said, "Mesha I know you did not call your sister that fast." She stopped me and said, "Nene, your brother just got shot!" I screamed, "What!" Right then and there I knew it was Junya! I asked Mesha which brother and she confirmed it was Junya. I took the phone away from my ear for a second, because I did not want to hear what she was telling me. Then I heard a soft voice that said, "Make peace I took him!" I started screaming and yelling saying, "No! No! Not my baby!" I did not want to listen to that voice at the time. I did not want to believe it, so I put the phone on speaker phone and when I was about to ask Mesha what happened to him she said why are you screaming like he died. I did not tell her what I heard, because I wanted her to tell me he was alright. I just moaned holding my stomach like someone was punching me. I was just crying trying to figure out what was going on. Then I told her I would call her back.

I called my father and he answered. He immediately said, "I know baby I'm down the street I'm going to him now!" I said okay and calmed down a little. I told him to please call me as soon as possible when he got there to let me know if he was ok. He agreed and I hung up. I just kept holding my stomach because it was hurting so much. I felt so hopeless. I could not do anything but call everyone. I could not be there for him or with him. So many memories of what we talked about went through my head so fast. I did not want to believe it. I called Mesha back and she told me that the ambulance was working on him she heard. Then my mom called in, so I merged her in our call, and she said the same thing Thomesha said. I just kept saying, "Ma! Not my brother! Not my baby!! She said, "I know baby!" I wiped my tears because I was not going to believe it. I put them on speaker phone and went on Facebook to see if anyone was saying anything. I did not really see any results, so I posted the picture I took of him with my kids a couple weeks back with a caption that read, "BREATHE BRO! YOU PROMISED"!

Then I told my mother and sisters I would call

them back, because I needed to call my father. I hung up with them, then called my father. He answered and hung up quickly. Right then I knew he was gone. I called him back and was crying saying, "Daddy is he okay!" He said, "No baby you brother is gone!" I started yelling and screaming, "No, No, No, No!" I kept screaming and screaming. My children came running and I kept screaming. I could not speak I just kept crying and screaming. I fell on the couch kicking and screaming. "Why did this happen? Why God? Why God? Why him? Why now?" I could hear Junya's voice in my head and the things we just said to each other. It kept me crying! I was angry with God! I was angry with everything! I was so angry! So, hurt and so lost! I did not know what to do. I kept seeing him get shot! It was too much for me.

My neighbors were pounding at my door asking what is wrong. I kept screaming and screaming, so my oldest daughter answered the door. They were asking me what happened, and I could not speak. My daughter told them what happened. I could not breathe, and they were trying to calm me down. They asked where my fiancé was. My daughter told them at the store. They opened my phone and called him. They told him to hurry, because of the situation. I was just yelling and screaming. "Why! Why! Why! My baby!" One of my neighbors which was my babysitter took my kids next door to her house so they would not see me that way. I was so hurt that nothing mattered at the time. I just kept screaming and yelling.

"How could this happen? I just spoke to you! Bro

you promised me! Why you do not listen? Why? Why? Why?" My hurt turned into angry so quickly. I wiped my tears and got so angry and said, "Who did this to my little brother?" I gained strength and call everyone to try to find out. I was told it was the same guy that Junya had problems with. I got even more angry and started yelling and screaming all over again. I was exhausted. I was hopeless. I did not want to hear any of the things people would normally say when someone died. I just wanted to talk to my brother again. I remembered asking God what he wanted from me. I surrendered my entire life to him. I went to church and studied his word (Bible). I forgave everyone that I felt hurt me and I forgave myself for any bad or harmful things I did. I asked him how he let this happened knowing my brother was trying to change everything for the best. I got no answer. I started screaming at God in my mind saying, "Where is the voice now? Where are the answers to my questions? Speak to me!" I was so frustrated! So tired of being good and trying to live right. I was angry! I wanted revenge for my brother at that moment! Through all those thoughts and feelings, I was still screaming and crying.

Then my fiancé walked in with something in his hands. He laid it on top of the sofa and rushed over to me. My neighbor that was with me said she was going to go check on the children while my fiancé stayed and made sure I was okay. He grabbed me and I just fell out in his arms and said, "They took him! They took my baby bro!" He was confused. He asked who took him and I said, "God took him!" He held me tight and I kept screaming. I continue to cry and cry as my stomach kept cramping. I stood up to catch my breath but kept kneeling over to hold my stomach. He stood there and held me. He kept saying he was sorry and that he knew how much he meant to me. I did not want to hear that. I just kept asking why. He said let us go to the kitchen and get you some water. I said okay. When I turned to walk to the kitchen as he helped me, I saw a game he brought with him must be when he was at the store, that laid on top of the sofa. It read, "Bibliopoly". When I wiped my eyes and really read the name on it while holding my stomach. I heard that voice again. It said, "Are you done?" I rolled my eyes and walked into the kitchen because I did not want to hear anything the voice was saying to me.

I went into the kitchen and held onto the counter as my fiancé poured me some water. Then I started crying again saying he was just here in the kitchen with me. How did this happen! I grabbed my stomach again and my fiancé caught me, thinking I was going to fall. He said, "Babe you have to drink this water and try not to get to upset, because you are going to be sick. I gave him an evil stare and said I am sick. I said, "I am sick of being good and trying to live right. I am sick of everything. My brother is gone just like that he was taking from me." My fiancé said, "He is not gone. He never left. He is with you." Then he walked out the kitchen.

At that moment it was like some sort of angel was speaking to me. Telling me to resurrect my brother through calling out his name. Then I heard my aunts voice telling me that when she gets upset, she just lifts her hand and call out Jesus name and it soothes her. I dropped my head in exhaustion. Then the voice said again, "Are you done!" It was like I just gave in to a fight and lost. I lift my hands and said, "Yes!" I called out Jesus name over and over as I lift my hands upward near my waist. I felt calm. Then I heard call out Junya's name. I called it about nine times in sets of three. Now when I say I hear this voice talking to me I do not mean this loud voice of a man. It is a thought guiding me in some way if that makes sense. Guiding my intuition into a voice I could hear. Guiding my spirit to feel what I could not see. The ninth time I heard Junya whisper in my right ear.

He said, "Don't cry big sis! I'm right here!" At that moment I thought I was going crazy to hear that. I thought maybe I was just hearing what he said before he left me in New York. So, I spoke back to see if it was him. I said, "Bro! You here!" He said, "Yes sis I'm here." I said, "Bro they are saying that you died and that someone killed you!" He said, "I know! They don't understand yet, but they will!" I said, "Okay bro just don't leave me please! Just stay with me and keep talking to me. He said he promised me he would never leave. I dried my tears and started smiling. I kept talking to him in the kitchen. I was so happy he was with me. If someone would have told me that this could have happened a month before I would have thought, they were crazy.

At that time, I did not care what people thought I was simply happy I could hear him. I told him to stay with me over and over just to hear him say, "I'm not leaving!" He said he was going to need my help with some things. I told him I would do anything just tell me and I would do it. My fiancé walked into the kitchen and looked at me as if he saw a ghost. He said, "Are you okay!" I said, "Yes, why!" He said because I looked so happy out of nowhere. I was afraid to tell him that Junya was there because I did not know how he would react, and I did not want anyone to tell me he was not there. My soul felt like I could tell him, so I did. When I told him, he did not look, or act surprised at all. He just said, "I told you he didn't leave." Then he started telling me his outlook on death. I learned so much in that forty minutes that we spoke about death and what Junya told me. Then I said well I have work to do, because he is going to need my help. He said okay.

I said let us grab the kids and call it a night because I was tired. He went to get the kids from our neighbor and brought them home. I bathe, fed them, and put them to bed. My family was calling me on the phone, so I answered them to assure them I was okay, and I would talk to them the next day. I went into the bedroom and got into bed and told God how sorry I was for the things I said. I asked for forgiveness. I thanked him for allowing me peace in all this and allowing me to communicate with Junya. I told Junya I loved him, and we will talk tomorrow. I said to him again not to leave me and he kept saying he promised, and he loved me.

Chapter 4: VISIONS

The next morning February 6, 2020, I felt great considering the situation that occurred, because I was still speaking with my brother. Everyone was terribly upset and sad. I was sad also, but Junya would not allow me to be that way for a second. Every time my mind shifted there, and I was going to cry he would tell me that he was there. So, I just kept my head up high because my brother told me he needed me, and I had to be strong for him. My oldest daughter woke up incredibly sad crying about Junya, so I sat her down and told her about our communication. I also told her that he did not want us to be sad because he is incredibly happy where he is at. I told her I do not believe death as we have been taught. I explained some of the things he needed me to do and told her that she could always talk to him if needed.

After I finished communicating and calming D'ziyah down I got on the phone to make some phone calls about the funeral and travel arrangements. I spoke to my father first. He told me that Junya's mother wanted to hold the funeral on his son's 1st birthday which was February 9, 2020. I was confused why she chose that date but agreed and called my mother and sisters to tell them and see what our travel arrangements were to get to South Carolina in such a short noticed. My mom three-way my sisters into the phone call. We all decided it was best if we drove since it was so much of us and the funeral was in three days. My mother and all my sisters wanted to go and support Junya because he was my brother, he meant a lot to them all, and he always made sure they had a good time when they traveled to South Carolina. We agreed to rent vehicles for the travel, so we booked the vehicles for pick up on February 7, 2020 at 9 a.m. After we decided about the travel arrangements, my mother said we would all leave New York at 12 p.m. on February 7, 2020 so we could arrive in South Carolina on February 8, 2020 at 12 a.m. giving us enough time to view his body and make it to the funeral. After we planned what we had to do to get moving we hung up the phone.

Shortly after that phone call my youngest aunt came to my house to support me during my time of need. We talked and I told her I was doing okay, because I was speaking to Junya and he reassured me he was happy and okay. Then she told me she wanted to go with us down south and she could help me drive.

I called my mother to see if that was possible and we made it happened. So, we all had to pack and get ourselves together. Before my aunt left, I asked her if she could watch my children while I went to the store to pick up some last-minute things for the trip, because my fiancé was at work. She agreed and I left.

When I got in the car the first thing, I said to Junya was, "Okay bro, now I'm alone tell me what you need me to do." As I drove around the corner to the shopping area where I took him on his visit. I passed the store that we went to together to buy his shinny shoes and I got kind of sad. I told him how much he loved those shoes. He laughed and agreed with me. He said, "Don't be sad big sis and this is not a funeral. This is my last performance, and it is going to be big, so do not dress in all black like it's a funeral." I said, "Okay bro, so what do you want me to wear?"

As I walked past that store and went unto the escalator of Burlington Coat Factory Junya said, "Get what you were going to get the other day for yourself." At that moment I thought, "how did he know about that?" I just told him that it was a couple days before, and usually when you go back for something you cannot find it. He said, "It's there sis, you just have to look all over for it." So, I went around my size area and found the entire outfit in my size just as Junya said. I took the outfit and the shoes to match to the dressing room. When I stepped out the dressing room and went to look in the mirror, I asked Junya how I looked. He said the outfit looked perfect for the celebration. I agreed and changed back into my original clothes I came into the store with and headed to the cash register to pay.

While I was walking there, I heard him say go back to the shoes. I asked him why because the shoes I found went perfect with the outfit I had. When I got no response from him, I ran over to the shoe section, because I wanted to hear his voice again. When I got there, I looked around for what he was trying to show me. Now I wear a size 10 in women's shoes, and it was not that many shoes for that size in Burlington Coat Factory, so I did not have to look that much before I noticed it. On a shelf with other shoes, but it seemed like the other shoes were moved away from what Junya was trying to show me, was a shiny pair of Calvin Klein size 10 heels with silver glitter all over it, which reminded me of the shoes Junya purchased from the other store. When I saw them, I grabbed my mouth and yelled to the top of my lungs in disbelief, "BROOOOOO-OOO!" Tears filled my eyes because I could not believe what I was seeing. I never saw those shoes in that store before and I was always in there. Then I heard his voice again laughing and saying to get those too. Everyone was looking at me like I was insane, but I did not care because my brother was with me. I grabbed the shoes and held them so close to me as I walked to the front to purchase them. Tears kept falling and I kept smiling and talking to him.

After I purchased the shoes and left the store, I went to a children's store to get outfits for my children to wear and went home. I was so excited about the shoes that I told my aunt, and I posted a picture of them on Facebook. My aunt could not believe it too. Then she left and went home to get packed and ready for the following day. I called Liliane (my friend) to tell her about what happened to my brother and how I would not be able to make it to church that Sunday of the celebration. She told me she would come over to my house that same day to pray with me and help me pack. I agreed and we hung up the phone. I called my fiancé and told him about my day and to see if he would be accompanying me for this journey down south. He got some vacation time to come with me and everything was falling into place without not much of a worry for me.

Later that evening I cooked and washed up all the children for bed. I knew my fiancé was tired, so I told him to get some rest while I cleaned and pack our stuff. He and the baby went to get some sleep. Then I received a phone call around 11 p.m. and it was Liliane apologizing for being late due to complications of her day and asking if I still wanted her to come over. I told her I would love it if she still came, because I still had a lot to do and I could use the company. When she arrived, she gave me a huge hug apologizing about my brother. I told her I was okay, and he was doing great, so I did not have to worry. She then realized I had a lot to do and asked if she could help.

My two oldest daughters came out their rooms because they could not sleep and asked if they could help as well. So, I asked Liliane to take out my youngest daughter hair while me and my oldest daughter fold up some clothes that we were going to pack. After we organized, fold the clothes, talked, and laughed Liliane was done Heaven's hair, so I sent them to bed because it was 2 a.m. and they needed rest. I still had a long way to go though. I needed to pack the clothes away and clean the kitchen and living room of the mess I made. I told Liliane she could go home, but she refused. She told me that when there is death in the family of her culture, they helped each other until everything was done, and the person was feeling okay spiritually and emotionally, then they went home.

She is from Congo, Africa. She said all of Africa does things that way. I told her that is an amazing way of doing things. I thanked her and asked her if she was hungry. She said yes, so I woke my fiancé up and asked him if he wanted anything because we were going to the store. He asked if we wanted him to go, but I told him no because we needed the air. So, we went to the store across the street brought us some sandwiches and chips. Went back into the house ate our food and talked. I told Liliane about communicating with my brother and understanding death differently. Then she called her husband (our preacher) because he wanted to talk to me.

After they spoke briefly, she handed me the phone and told me he wants to share some things with me. When I put the phone to my ear and said hello, the preacher asked me how I was doing. I told him I was doing great and was happy his wife was with me, because I needed her support. He apologized for not being there and I told him that I understood. We prayed together and he shared something that God told him prior to speaking to me. He said God was using me a servant to the people that I love and the people that love Junya. He told me that even though I may not feel strong enough to carry everyone, God is going to help me. He said I would stand out and the people would listen to me when I spoke. God would make sure of it. All I had to do was listen and follow the voice inside to bring peace and love to this situation. He told me a lot of people is hurting and need what I am sent to do.

I thanked him for that word and told him that I got that message early that morning. I knew God was inside of me and using my spirit and intuition to guide me through everything, so hearing it from another person that was not present with me through this time was reassurance. We said another prayer and he told me he loved me and to have safe travels. Then I gave the phone back to Liliane.

While they talked for a little longer, I remember looking at her in disbelief of everything that was going on and then a sense of strength came over me. I was ready for this journey and I knew why I was chosen. She hung up the phone, we put the rest of the clothes away, and she helped me clean the house spotless as we continued to talk. Then I called her a cab and we prayed together. When we prayed my body was numbed. I felt a spirit take over me and I could hear it talking to me clearly telling me I could do this. Tears ran down my face as I held Liliane hand in prayer and just listened. I felt so much love and peace.

I knew she was leaving, but it felt like I was taking her spirit with me to South Carolina. It was an amazing feeling and I thought to myself that that was the reason why we connected so well the way we did. I walked Liliane to the elevator because she would not let me walk her downstairs. I gave another huge hug and kiss on the cheek and thank her again for coming. I told her I could do this journey and I wanted her to call or text me when she got home safely so I would know. I went inside and thanked God for everything all over again. I told my brother I was ready for whatever he needed from me and I will see him soon. It was about 4 a.m. and I had to wake up at 6 a.m. so I laid next to my fiancé softly and went to sleep after Liliane text me she was home.

The next day on February 7, 2020 I woke up a little late at 7 a.m. I took a shower and got some coffee. Then I called my aunt to make sure her and her children were ready for me to pick them up before getting the rental car. I knew I would not have time after so we decided before would be better. I was happy. I got into the car and jammed my favorite Gospel CD by Jason Breland called, **Thank You for Loving Me**. I arrived at my aunt's house and we all went to meet my sister at the rental place. We arrived there about 8:30 a.m. which was perfect for what we had booked it for. When I parked, I had a vision of me driving my own car down south, but I did not really pay attention to it because I knew I was getting a rental car.

When I entered the building and gave them my information along with my sister, they pulled our vehicles that we booked along the front then asked us for our payments. I handed the guy that was doing my case my debit card and he told me that they only excepted credit cards. I told them that I never used credit cards and he apologized and said it was company policy. I asked my sister about it and she said she had a credit card to get hers, but she needed to add more money to get the huge vehicle that they needed. I asked the guy if my sister could get my rental for me and he said no because there could only be one license per vehicle. I got upset and worried. I tried calling my mother, but she was on her way from Connecticut where she lived to meet us in New York. I asked my other sister, and she did not use credit cards either. I was truly angry and lost on what to do. Then I stood aside everyone and prayed then I suddenly calmed down.

I went outside to talk to my aunt, and she told me she had the same vision of me taking my own car, but she did not want to say anything because I wanted a rental. I called my mother and asked her if it would still be enough room for my aunt if I took my own car. She said they would have room for two of her children because my oldest sister would not be accompanying us because she had to work. Everything worked out perfect. I apologized to the guy for the inconvenience and got into my car to go back home leaving my aunt with my younger sister. Then my younger sister told me to wait, because the bank was taking an awfully long time transferring the money to her credit card and she did not want me to leave just in case everything did not go as plan, and I needed to take my aunt with me. So, I stayed with them. It took about an hour and a half. We went to McDonalds for something to eat and I gassed up my vehicle.

When my sister received the phone call that everything was ready, she got the rental and parked her personal vehicle on the side of the street near the rental place. We did not leave the rental place until 11:30 a.m. I called my mother to tell her we should leave out at 1 p.m. to give me and my family some time to get dressed. I arrived at home to get everything ready and get dressed. While we were putting everything into our vehicle it started raining a lot. We were getting soaked so I pulled the vehicle as close as I could to our building. My mom, sisters, and aunt were pulling up in their huge truck as we were packing the vehicle. My aunt and her youngest daughter of her children got out my mother's vehicle and into mines and my two daughters rode with my mother and sisters for more leg room. After everyone got situated, I said a prayer and we all started on our journey at about 2 p.m.

I offered to drive first and told my aunt to rest. I followed behind Thomesha (second younger sister) and got lost as soon as we got to New Jersey. I just put on my GPS on and continued driving. They called and asked where we were and I told them to just continue, because we would eventually catch up. I was determined to get there so nothing was going to stop me from getting to my brother. I drove for the first ten hours. Out of the ten hours. When I was not listening to the gospel CD, I was listening to 90's love music while looking into the sky.

The sky was changing in every state, but each state

it looked as though Junya was following me. The way the sky looked I have never seen anything like it before. It looked like the clouds was opening and light rays were reaching down to Earth taking spirits to Heaven. I was so amazed. When the sky was not that way it was dark. Not a scary type of dark though. Nothing seemed scary to me at that point anymore. Especially after it would seem to other people that I was talking to a ghost. It was not that way though. It was my spirit communicating with the soul of Junya. If you would have told me this would happen a year prior, I would not believe you either, or I would probably think the whole thing was crazy. I felt as if I was going through a spiritual awakening or something. I did not let my mind wonder off from the way I was feeling.

I had a vision of me speaking at my brother's celebration. It was so beautiful and peaceful. I was afraid, but it felt destined. I pictured me near the back of the church when they called me. I walked up to his body and took my shiny shoes off placing them near his coffin, then walked up on the stage and started speaking. I did not know what I was saying, but I knew it helped a lot of people with all the emotions they felt inside by the incident. I knew because when I investigated the crowd, they started crying first, then they started laughing, then they started smiling looking up. I told my aunt and husband my vision and that I had to speak at the celebration. I was so happy and knew I needed to speak at the celebration, so I called me and Junya's younger sister to ask. When I got her on the phone and asked her, she said that only one person could speak because the situation was too difficult to handle. I was a little upset, but I understood where she was coming from. When I hung up the phone, I said a silent prayer and said out loud, "God if you make a way I would follow." I kept having that vision for a while, so I knew it was going to happen.

I also had another vision while driving that I shared with my aunt and fiancé prior to arriving in South Carolina. God told me that I had to visit the crime scene where my brother had been shot. Everything I heard or saw inside I would question it to see if I would receive an answer. When I did not, I knew I just had to complete the assignment to see what the answer was. I questioned this vision asking why I would need to go there. I was told I needed to go there to see what happened for myself, so I do not get affected by what others said that happened. I was also told that I would gain the power to pray over people that were hurting to calm them down. God told me that I would have to open my hands over the spot where he died to see the vision, then close my hands to gain the power of prayer and healing.

My last vision was of me praying with his mother. Junya told me everything he wanted me to say to her, so she would know he was okay. He told me specific things to say in prayer with her and when I heard them, I saw her face looking at me as though she would know I was in communication with Junya from something only her and him spoke about. After I received those visions and listened to my music, I did not even notice that I drove for ten hours. I remember saying to Junya aloud, "I told you bro the first time you asked me to drive to South Carolina that I was not going to do it but look at me now. You always know how to get me out of my comfort zone, and I love you for that." I started laughing out loud. Then we stopped and took a thirty-minute break and filled up our gas tank. We also brought more food and my aunt drove the rest of the way.

We arrived in Georgetown, South Carolina about 4 a.m. on Saturday February 8, 2020. We all stayed at my grandmother's house. When we arrived, we spoke to our grandmother, unpacked our clothes, ate some leftover pizza, and went to bed. We woke up a couple of hours later at 9 a.m. My grandmother made my favorite breakfast of fried Roger Wood sausage, scrambled eggs, and homemade cheese grits. We all ate and talked. Then I asked my fiancé to ride with me to go to Walmart and grab some small things that was needed. We got dressed and asked my grandmother to watch the kids while we went to the store. We went to Walmart, which helped us spend a little time alone together and talk about how I felt. I told him I felt good and I was ready for everything. I thanked him for coming with me and supporting me. I knew I would need him to help me stay strong. I knew if no one believed me, he did and no matter what he would have my back. He helped coach me through every step. When we left Walmart and was almost to my grandmother's house, I asked my fiancé to come with me to the crime scene. It was just three minutes away from my grandmother's house. He agreed.

Chapter 5: The Bigger Picture

When we arrived at the crime scene my fiancé guarded me and our surroundings as I walked to the gate and lift my right hand and put it on the gate. He is always overprotective of me, but I was not afraid of anything happening to me, because I could feel nothing was going to happen. When I raised my right hand, placed it on the gate, and closed my eyes I asked my brother what he wanted me to see. I saw the entire story. Then I opened my eyes and walked around the building with my fiancé telling him the story that I saw. It was like I saw the bigger picture of what happened, where my brother was mentally when it all happened, and how he tried to stop what was happening. I saw my brother trying to stop the beef that they had with one another by talking to the guy. My brother then realized that no matter what he said to the guy he still wanted beef with him. My brother then ran to get away from the guy and the guy shot twice and one bullet hit my brother. He fell instantly to the ground and the guy ran and got in the car to leave. What I saw next is when things really got weird. As my brother laid on the ground he was not alone. I saw someone holding him and I heard the car spin off.

I followed the car in the vision with my eyes and heard the conversation that the killer and driver had. I even heard what the killer was saying and thinking in his mind. The driver wanted to know why he shot him. It was as though he thought the murderer only was supposed to rob him not shoot him. The murderer told him that my brother only got hit once and that he would live, and they would be fine, but my brother would not want no beef after that. So right then it was as if the murderer did not expect my brother to die. Then I heard the murderer mind speaking. It was as if God tried to stop him prior to him even reaching my brother, but all he could think about was the viral video, Junya's success, robbing Junya one last time, and making a song about him shooting Junya. That jealousy, envy, and anger overpowered the last choice he had prior to going to Junya. I saw Junya lying on the ground bleeding out as help came and he was talking to God the entire time. He was sad and peaceful at the same time. He was tired and afraid of dying, but his angels spoke back to him.

Then I dropped my head in disbelief of all the things I saw, and I heard that I must forgive them for what they did to my brother, so I could bring peace. I did not know how to feel at that moment. I did not know what to say. It was as if I was stuck. I missed my brother so much. I was so proud of him for trying to stop everything, but I wished he were still alive. Then I heard Junya say, "I tried Big Sis!" I started telling him that I knew, and I was so proud of him and I knew he was tired of everything. I told him to rest and I would take it from there just tell me what to do and I will do anything. That part hurt so much, but I knew I had to be strong for my city and my little brother. I dropped my head and started praying. God told me to lift my hand to the gate and pray so I could gain the power to pray over the people that love Junya. Then I was told to close my hand. When my fiancé saw that, he asked me if I had what I needed, and I told him I did. We got into the car and headed back to grandmother's house to get ready to view his body.

When we parked and walked through the yard, I saw my mother. She told me what was said that happened to Junya and I disagreed with her and told her another story. She said that what I told her was wrong and asked me where I heard my story from. I said Junya told me. Then she disagreed, but I just said okay. because I knew what I had just saw and one day the truth would come out. While going to get ready to go to the viewing, my best friend called me and said she was coming over to go with me. Her name is Jasmine Greene. She has been my best friend since we were about five years old. Even though I lived thousands of miles away from her we always kept in touch and whenever I came to South Carolina she would meet me where I was so I could spend time with her. She also knew my little brother and wanted to support me and him. She means the world to me and is always there when I need her.

We all got dressed and Jasmine showed up just in time. We got into our vehicles and started on our journey to where Junya was being held at. The entire car ride was quiet as though everyone was trying to see how I would react. Plus, it was a bitter moment for us all. I was in a much happier place at that time, so I just played my Jason Breland gospel CD the whole way and talked to Junya. I remember Junya telling me not to worry I am strong enough for this. God told me that I would not cry before I got to South Carolina. I knew I would not cry if Junya stayed with me and I could hear his voice. I just kept smiling knowing he was there. God told me that he gave me the power to pray over people if they were crying and they would calm down. I was told to place one hand behind their head and one behind their back and hug them as I pray. Right then I knew what my assignment was other than going to see my brother.

As we drove in the parking lot of the church where they held Junya's body, a sense of excitement came over me as I told Junya a loud that I made it. I said, "I'm here bro! We made it! I can't wait to see you!" When I parked the car, my family kept asking me if I was okay. I just smiled and said I was ready. I let my mother take my two oldest daughters and sisters inside as I stayed with Jasmine, my aunt Twequette, my fiancé, and my baby Royal. I told all of them that we must grab hands and pray prior to going inside. So, we did just that. After the prayer I felt stronger and even happier. I felt like I could do anything that was needed of me and not be afraid. We entered the building and heard people crying softly.

Everyone in my family went to see Junya before me to view the body, as I stood back and talked to God. When I walked on the carpet to view Junya's body it was as if he was not dead. It seemed like I was at a red-carpet event for him. I was smiling so hard with that vision inside my head. I walked up to the front near the casket slowly. My mother met me in the middle and placed her hands around me and asked me if I was ready. It was as if she thought I was upset or was going to be upset. I told her I was ready as we walked to the front.

When we got to the front of the church where his body laid, and I could see his face I stopped. My mother whispered in my ear and said, "Come on baby I got you." My mother gave my back a little push and my body froze. Then she grabbed my arm and tried to pull me gently. I looked at her with a smile and asked her if I could do it on my own. She said yes and sat down. She told me she would be close if I needed her. When she walked away, I started talking to God. I said, "Okay God, it's me and you. You told me I would not cry, and I trust you fully. Help me with this please." I took a deep breath, put a smile on my face, and walked up to my brother. When I got to him, I smiled and told him face to face everything that I always told him. I also told him that I knew what he tried to do, and I am so proud of him. I told him that he could rest and did not have to feel the way he did before or look over his shoulder because God had him. I told him how much I love him and how I love that suit that he wore. I told him that I was still mad about him for not sending my clothes that I wanted, but I was happy about the sweater he gave me off his back. Then I told him that Fiancé came with me and I would like him to meet him. I turned around to find Kayheim (my fiancé) and called him up to Junya. I introduced him to Junya.

He spoke to Junya apologizing about not meeting him sooner, and he would always remember what they spoke about on the phone. Then he went and sat down as I spent a couple more minutes alone with Junya, I told Junya to stay with me and watch over us. I said, "Bro now you could be everywhere at one time watching over everyone." When I turned around to go and sit with my family, they were staring at me as though they thought I was going to cry. I walked over to them smiling and my daughter was crying. I whispered in her ear and told her to remember what we spoke about. I told her that Junya is okay and he was still talking to me. Then I looked in her eyes and told her to look in mines as I smile with no tears knowing he was ok. After that she dried her eyes and started smiling. I could see that she believed me. Then I turned to my younger sister Rella and asked her if she was okay. She said she was, but I knew she was not. She was still in shock, but Junya told me not to worry about her because he would talk to her as soon as she let him. I told her Junya is okay and she would soon know it. I looked in her eyes as I spoke to her and she calmed down a little. Then I sat down in front of her for what seemed like only two minutes before I heard someone screaming loud crying.

My spirit told me to stand up and go to them. I told my family I would be right back and walk over to the person I heard screaming. The whole time I was not afraid because it felt as if I knew what to do, even though I never did anything like this before. When I got to her, I noticed it was a cousin of mines from my father's side that was screaming while sitting and my father's sister was holding her as she was yelling. I kneeled to her and told her it was going to be okay.

She just kept yelling and screaming that this was not supposed to happen. I listened to her as she let it all out. I was so calm, and I could not believe it. Then I placed my hand on her shoulder and tried to calm her down. I asked her to look at me so she would know who I was. When she saw it was me, she grabbed me and cried some more asking why Niqua. That was a name she used to call me when I was little. I asked her to look at me again. I told her I knew how she felt and Junya wants her to know that he is okay.

Then I heard my spirit say grab and hug her and start praying. I did not know what to pray about and my spirit told me to just talk to God and leave the rest up to them. So, I asked her if I could pray with her. She looked at me and said I could. So, I hugged her and placed one hand behind her head and the other on her back. I started talking to God, and I could not hear what was coming out of my mouth. It was weird. I even asked God what I was saying to her and my spirit told me not to worry, it would help her calm down. It was amazing, the communication and the feeling that I was feeling all at the same time. I could feel her body calming down second by second. It was unbelievable, and I felt as though I did not really do anything. Then she just stopped crying. I said, "Amen!" Then I looked at her and told her everything would be okay and soon she will know it. I told her again that Junya is okay, and he is still here. She just must calm down and talk to him, then listen. "He will speak back to you", I said to her. I looked into her eyes and grabbed her face while smiling and said trust me. She shook her head, and I knew she believed me.

I heard other people crying out loud and my spirit sent me to them to do the same thing as well. Then I saw our niece and nephew of our younger sister from our father's side that loved Junya so much walk into the building crying. I thought at that point I was going to cry, because I know how little kids could break you down with their crying. As I walked to them, I asked Junya to help me with them, he told me do not worry because I was strong, and I would not cry.

Then a little girl ran up to me before I reached them and gave me a huge hug. I did not know who she was, but she had Junya's name on all her clothes including her socks and hairbow. I grabbed her and pick her up as I continue to walk towards our niece and nephew. I stopped and prayed over her and put her down. Then I asked our niece and nephew's mother if I could pray over her children. She told me she was proud to see me in the spirit I was in. She apologized about my little brother because she knew how much I loved him, and he loved me. I thanked her and looked at the children. I kneeled and grabbed the little boy and stood up placing one hand behind his head and one on his back. I started talking to God and could feel his little body calming down. It amazed me every time it happened.

When I kneeled to put the boy back on the ground my spirit told me to look him in his eyes and tell him that Junya was okay and he loved him very much. When I did that, I saw a big smile come upon his face as if he knew. It was beautiful and gave me more strength as I picked up our niece to do the same thing for her. When I was done, they both were calm and ready to walk forward to see their uncle. I gave their mother a hug and told her that Junya was okay and I loved her very much.

As they walked away that same little girl ran into my arms again and gave me a huge hug. Her spirit was amazing and calming to me. It was as if a light were surrounding her and I could feel it when she hugged me. I gave her another big hug then asked her where her mother was. She pointed behind me, so I turned around and walked to where she showed me. When I got in front of her mother, I continued to hold her as I asked her mother if that was her child. Then the lady looked up at me and I noticed that she was the mother of Junya's son. I opened my arms and gave her a huge hug as she cried, and I told her that I apologized about what happened to Junya. Then I told her that Junya must really love her daughter because she kept running to me as if she knew me. She told me he did, even though that was not his daughter he always made her feel as if she was.

I told her that Junya is okay and if she calms down and talk to him then he would answer her. I also said that he was all around us making sure we were good. I told her he said he would never leave us. Then she started crying with her head down in disbelief. I lift her head up and asked her if I could pray for her. She shook her head yes. I continued to hold her daughter and placed one of one of my hands behind her back bringing her close to me. I started talking to God and

Junya asking for them to reassure her about what I was saying. I remember also asking them for her strength as she and her children walked their journey without Junya physically. She started to calm down and I continued to talk to God and Junya a little longer because I knew she would need it. After I ended the prayer, I looked at her and told her no matter what was needed for her children that she was to reach her out to me. I would be there for her always. She smiled and hugged me again. Then I handed her daughter to her and hugged them both and told them I loved them. I asked her where my nephew was, and she assured me that I would see him the next day at the funeral. I told her that it was not to be considered a funeral but a celebration, because Junya was going to show up and show out just like he always does. Then I blinked my right eye at her and she started smiling.

After that, my spirit said everything was fine and I could go! So, I walked over to my family and asked if everyone was ready to go. They agreed! We took a couple of photos together knowing how much Junya loved people taking photos and we went to our cars. While we are driving back to my grandmother's house, I told Junya I did it all for him. I thanked him and God for staying with me and guiding me through everything. Then I told them that if they make a way for me to speak at the celebration the next day I would.

When we arrived at my Grandmother's house, I found out that a candlelight would be held for Junya at the crime scene location twenty minutes after our arrival. I freshened up and drove my best friend home and went to the candlelight. Kayheim traveled with me and my aunt stayed with all the children. When we got to the candlelight people were standing around a fire with lit candles in their hands. We joined the circle, and someone brought us candles. We lit our candles and watch different people say different stories of how my brother touched their lives. I noticed a couple of people from school when I was younger and lived in South Carolina.

One younger white boy that did not look familiar, but his story that he told when he got to the fire touched my soul. He introduced himself as Caleb and he pointed at a woman and said that was his mother. He said they were homeless and one day they met Junya and he gave them money. Junya also paid for them a hotel for one week and gave Caleb his number and told him that if there was anything, they needed to call him. Caleb said he spoke to Junya often and he always lift his spirit. He said he will deeply miss Junya and he thank him for everything. I was so shocked to hear his story of my brother. I knew Junya was that way but standing there hearing different people reassure me was even more amazing. I spoke after them telling Junya I was so proud of him and how much I love the man he was. Then Rella spoke after me. We all said our goodbyes to Junya and Rella pulled Caleb and his mother to the side. I walked to them as well. We invited them to our grandmother's house to meet the rest of our family while we ate oysters and blue crabs by the fire.

We all went around the corner to my grandmother's house and they came along with us. They told the rest of the family who they were and what Junya did for them. My family accepted them with open arms. Another one of my childhood friends that lost a brother a couple months before named Laquarius Ford joined us as well for support. My mother and her mother were friends when we were younger and lived in South Carolina. We spent many years together and did not lose touch even when moved to New York. We laughed and joked about old times and she apologized about my brother. We both spoke about some good times we had with our brothers. Everyone was having a great time, but something was missing. It was my oldest brother, two younger sisters, and my father that lived near my grandmother in the area. I got on my phone and called my little sisters and they told me they were already with my father and our big brother was on his way. That was perfect because they all could come over, so I invited them.

While we started setting up the fire in the backyard of my grandmother's house, my mother came and told me that my father had arrived. I went to meet them at the door and found out he brought some of my uncles and cousins that I never met with him. I was happy. It was a lot of them. My father introduced me to all of them and then we all started eating oysters and having a great time. It was such a wonderful time. I felt so peaceful. I remember telling Junya to look at what he did by bringing everyone together on both sides of my family for the first time. I thanked him so much. Then one of my sisters from my mother's side showed up with her father and my mother introduced him to everyone. Everyone was having a great time drinking beer and champagne while eating a ton of crabs and oysters. I looked for Rella to see if she was okay and I noticed her in the street with the jeep doors open playing Junya's favorite song while she was dancing in circles, and one of my sisters was video recording her. No one was crying or upset. We were all enjoying ourselves just the way Junya would want us to. He always made sure everyone was having a great time enjoying themselves while he was near. I loved that about him, and he still was doing a great job at it.

Me and my father was not in a great space at the time. I was upset with him before because he fell in love with someone remarkably close to me and hid it from me until after they had a baby together. I held a grudge on him for that, but prior to me coming to South Carolina I surrendered my life to fulfill the purpose I was set on Earth to do. Along with doing that I forgave him for everything, and I forgave myself for the feelings I held inside because of the situation, so it ended before I even took the trip. I never told my father I had forgiven him though, so that night was perfect to do it. Plus, I really miss my father a lot.

After a couple hours went by and it was time to clean up, I started washing the dishes and my father came inside the house to give me a hug because he was leaving. I wrapped my arms around him tight. The same way I did Junya. It felt great to hug my father after so many years of not hugging him and so many years of being angry. When I was about to let go of him my spirit would not let me. I held on tight for what seemed like an exceedingly long time. It felt like forever, but I think it was about twenty minutes. I could tell he needed that as well because he hugged me even tighter too. Our connection seemed like it got back just as tight as our hug. I told him I loved him so much and apologized for everything I have ever said wrong to him. He said the same thing to me and promise we were not going to that separate place anymore. He told me he loved me so many times, and I shed a tear knowing Junya was smiling at me. It felt like Junya was there hugging us too. Junya made everything possible and I was just so proud of him and I could not stop telling him that. Everyone was still talking and laughing. My mother was watching me and my father with a huge smile on her face. We cleaned the house completely and said our goodnights to each other, because we had a big day ahead of us the next day. It was the celebration of Junya!!

Chapter 6: Junya's Last Performance

The next morning, I woke up in a great mood. I started my day speaking with God and Junya telling them that I was ready for whatever was needed of me. I ask them to make a way and I will follow. Then I started to get all our clothes ready for our showers. My grandmother made breakfast for us and pulled me to the side, apologizing about not being able to make the celebration because my grandfather was sick and could not stay at home alone. I gave her a huge hug and told her it was okay. I thanked her for rushing to hospital when the incident happened to give us the information about Junya because we could not be there. I told her I love her very much. She told me to remain strong and everything would be okay.

We all ate our breakfast and one by one started taking our showers. All the girl got dressed and talked in the same room. I dressed my two younger daughters in white and gold dresses with gold shoes and gold jewelry. I did that because I knew how much Junya loved his gold color. My older daughter wore a white button-down top with grey and white slack pants with shiny silver heels. She wanted to wear them for her uncle Junya, and I agreed. Kayheim wore a navy-blue suit that I thought looked amazing. He said he would wear a suit for Junya, and I appreciated that so much from a person who really did not wear suits. I complemented him every chance I got. I wore the outfit me and Junya picked out, which was a powder pink dress with a long blazer like swede, cover with natural beige stockings. I wore the shiny shoes he led me to, but also took in my bag some powder pink pump heels and some black flip flops. Once everyone got dress, I got dressed last and my aunt asked me to do my makeup. I was so happy, but I told her not to put too much because I did not really wear makeup like that. It was worth wearing for my brother though. After everyone got dressed and did our makeup we started on our journey to the church where the celebration was being held.

    I played my Jason Breland- **Thank You for Loving Me** CD the whole ride, smiling and mediating talking to Junya while driving. My aunt and Kayheim rode with me and our babies rode in the jeep with us as well. While I was driving, I received another vision of me speaking at Junya's celebration again, but this time it was a little more detail revealed. I saw me leaving my shiny shoes inside his casket and I stood in front of his closed casket with my hands held up as if I were raising him or something. Then I turned my hands over his casket as if his soul were being given to me. After I saw that vision, I told Kayheim and my aunt that I just received confirmation that I was going to speak again.

    I told them that God would make a way and Junya was going to tell me when to open my mouth. After I told them that, I noticed a police car following me awfully close. I told my aunt to call my mother that rode in front of me and tell her to slow down, because of what was happening. She turned down a different street then where we were supposed to go, and they still were following me. At that moment I realized that

I was experiencing what my brother had told me about the police down there. He told me even if you were not doing anything, they would follow you very closely and you would become afraid. Then I heard my Rella saying on my mother phone that Junya told her what to do when they do that. She told me that my mother was going to turn at the next left and stop in someone's yard and I should follow them. I agreed and followed. When we turned and stop the police kept going. We waited there for about three minutes to see if they would circle around to come back but they did not, so my mother put on the GPS and we continued to the celebration. I started talking to Junya telling him that now I understood what he meant about the cops in South Carolina and I could not imagine how he was be treated as a black man driving alone.

    I began to play my CD again starting all over as we traveled the rest of the way. I silently talked to Junya inside and right before we pulled up to our destination, he said something that I thought was funny, and I knew he was looking out for my best interest. Junya told me that I should take of my natural stockings and just wear my pumps, because it got stained as I walked around with no slippers getting ready. He told me when I gave him my shoes people would see my stained stockings. We both started laughing. I said aloud, "Thanks for always looking out for me baby bro!" Then I told my fiancé and aunt what Junya said. I told them that when I stopped the car and my stocking were a little dirty, we all going to laugh. About five minutes after that we arrived at the church and park our car on the side of the street because it was no more room in the parking lot. Then I asked my fiancé to take off my shoes, so he came around to the driver's side and took them off and they were dirty. We all started laughing hard, because we knew Junya was making jokes on me and looking out for me at the same time. I close my door and took my stocking off in the car. I added lotion to my feet and put my shinny shoes back on. We all got out the car. Everyone was rushing across the street to the church to get a seat and I stood by the car talking to Junya telling him I could not believe how much people were there to watch him perform one last time.

He said, "That's not all big sis! There are a lot more coming they are just late, but they will make it." My mom then walked to me and told me to hurry because all his family was about to line up. My heart was racing fast as she hurried me. Then my heartbeat changed when I heard a voice say, "Everything has a divine time!" My entire body calmed down and I looked at my mother smiling with my hands opened and said, "Ma everything has a divine time!" She said okay and left me there. Junya then told me that that was his biggest performance, and everything had to be great. I agreed with him and told him to tell me what was needed for me and I would do it. He told me not to cry and keep smiling while I greeted people and thank them for coming.

I walked across the street to the church smiling with my hands raised near my side. It felt like I was flying as the wind pushed me towards the people. I met up with my family and fiancé. I took my baby from my fiancé's arm to hold her for a while. One of my youngest brothers from my father's side that I have not seen since we were younger walked up and spoke to me. I handed my baby back to my fiancé and gave my brother the biggest hug. I told him what seemed like a million times that I loved him, missed him, and was so happy to see him again. His name is Marcus Brown. He is my second youngest brother. I introduced him to my fiancé, and they hugged each other as well. Then my fiancé told me to go and be with the rest of Junya's family in the front and do what I came there to do. He told me he would stay with my family and our kids. I kissed him and told him I love him.

Then me and Marcus held hands as we walked towards the front of the church. I spoke to some of the people I knew, that also knew Junya and thanked them for coming. As me and Marcus continued to walk to the front Caleb and his mother walked up to me. I gave them a tight hug and took photos with them. I thanked them for coming and told them I was so happy to see them. Then my brother and I took photos as well. After that we continued to walk towards the front of the church and saw our two younger sisters standing in line. We joined them and gave them both a hug.

All the immediate family were told to come closer to the front of the line to sit in the front rows of the church, so we all walked to the lady that made the announcement. When we got to the front, we all were being split up, but Marcus continued to hold my hand. The lady that made the announcement were putting people in specific spots and it seemed as if we were being pushed back. I could tell people were getting aggravated because of it, but I just remained patient. One lady standing behind me that looked familiar pushed me a little and told me to go to the front, because I was Junya's sister and I should be in the front row. I smiled and looked back at her and said, "Everything has a divine time!" Shortly after we got into the church and we were placed in the third row. Everything looked so beautiful. Junya's casket was closed with an amazing set of flowers on top of them. The choir were in their beautiful robes singing a beautiful song. Me and Marcus sat next to each other. I sat on the edge of the pew near the aisle. My little sisters sat behind us.

I could hear people getting aggravated and other people crying without even turning my head. I tried to ignore all the frustration by looking at the choir and zoning everything out to stay in a peaceful place to focus on what needed to be done. I sat down staring at the choir smiling and singing with them, then I heard stand up. I stood up and looked around then noticed behind me that my little sister Zandrena from my father's side fell out after crying a lot. Everyone was panicking and I heard to put my hand over her and pray. I did just that calmly, then I told them to take her outside for air and she will be okay. I sat back down after that not worried, because I did not feel the need. I heard so many people getting angry and crying. It was as if I was zoning in and out. I looked at the choir for peace as they continued to sing through all the frustration. Only then were I able to focus to the voice that came from within me.

I heard stand up again, but this time with a lot of bass and what seemed like wind that forced me to stand up. I stood up and closed my eyes listening carefully. I heard arguing at the door and the security saying no one else was allowed inside the church because it was too pack. I heard so many people yelling out of anger of not being able to come inside. Then I heard Junya say, "Look around big sis!" I opened my eyes and looked around for what he was trying to show me. He told me that he would not want anyone to be left out of seeing his last performance. I said, "I know bro! What do you want me to do?" He said, "Go outside big sis!" I debated with him telling him I would lose my seat. He said loudly, "Go outside!" I asked Marcus to watch my bag and I started walking towards the front exit of the church. It was difficult because so many people were trying to get to their seats. After struggling to get past all the people, the security stopped me and told me that once I exit, I would not be able to come back inside. I told him I was okay with that because my brother needed me outside.

As soon as I step over the front door exit, I felt the presence of Junya. I smiled and took a deep breath as I raised my hands. My spirit told me to go to the left of the exit and I walked over smiling with my hands raised feeling the wind blowing me. I was told to look up and then I saw Junya in the sky. My spirit told me to tell him at that time everything I wanted to say to him. I said, "Broooooo! Hi!!! I love you so much!! I see you up there! Do not ever leave me please! I am so proud of you for everything!! Look at all these people who came out today to see you perform! They love you, bro! I love you, bro!" God told me to turn around. When I turned around everyone that was left in the parking lot surrounded me in what seemed like a large circle. I felt a power within me I never felt before. It was as if I could do anything. It felt like I was flying with Junya. I knew that was my vision before. That was where I was going to speak. He made a way and I felt it.

My spirit opened with trust and freedom. No ego or pride just love. It felt so amazing to feel that amount of love at one time. God told me to open my mouth and speak. I remember opening my arms and telling everyone I knew we could not get inside the celebration, but Junya was performing outside too. At that moment I zoned out to zone within myself and the spirit inside took completely over my body and voice. I started speaking to the spirit that was speaking to the people asking what was being said to them through me. Whatever was being said to the people I could feel their spirits inside their bodies calming down and relaxing as if the anger and frustration were no more. I also saw my aunts face in disbelief as tears rolled down her eyes. When I asked my spirit again what was being said I heard to just smile while looking left and looking right.

I could not believe what was happening because I could feel my mouth moving but saying something different from what me and my spirit was talking about. It was the most beautiful thing I have ever seen or felt. I felt Junya inside of me working with my spirit telling everyone what he wanted to say to them. I could feel the happiness within the hearts of the people from what was being said, but I could not hear. I thought I would cry, but it was not a sad feeling. I felt loved. I felt happiness. I felt free.

I zoned back into what felt like reality when I heard my spirit say, "Now tell the people what happened at Burlington Coat Factory." I zoned back in and began telling people what happened at Burlington. I told them how Junya led me to my shoes in detail. From the looks on their faces and the feeling I got from them all I knew they believed me. They were laughing and crying from what I told them. I made jokes about Junya telling me that the shoes would be comfortable, but they were not. So, I took them off in front of the people just like my vision and asked my aunt to grab my slippers. I was so happy to see them all smiling and filled with joy. I told them all how much I loved them and how thankful I was for them being there for my little brother. I told them that I wanted a hug from each one of them. I also told them that we must all show love to each other. I said, "Junya loves you guys so much. He is so happy you guys showed up and showed out at his last performance. It means the world to him and me. This is and will always be Junya's World!" I gave everyone a hug one by one and told them I love them. They all thanked me for coming outside to speak to them. They said that I really helped them look at things a different way. I spoke to a lot of my childhood peers that I knew from when I was younger, and I did not know they knew my little brother.

The celebration was over and all the people from

inside of the church flooded the parking lot. Junya's mother came outside and sat inside of the limo. I walked over to her and asked if I could pray with her. We grabbed hands in prayer and bowed our heads. It felt like Junya spoke through me to tell her everything he wanted her to know. When the prayer ended, I could feel it and we said Amen. I knew the message got through to her by the look on her face.

Then all the men started to bring Junya outside the church. I kept my eye on Junya's body the entire time for what Junya needed me to do next. His mother and our sister went on the right side of the church where he was being buried and sat at the burial site. When the guys started to carry him through the parking lot to the burial site, I told Junya to make a way for me to finish the vision I saw. At that very moment people were talking to me, but I saw no one walking behind the guys carrying Junya. I ran behind them with my daughter, then Caleb came and grabbed my other hand and followed. Together, I left all our hands as if we were helping carrying him, lifting my brother to the universe. I told Junya all the things I wanted to say to him. I started making funny jokes about him to keep everyone happy, because that is exactly what Junya liked to do. I told Junya I knew he was eating well in Heaven already because it looked like the men could barely carry him. We all started laughing and kept walking to the burial site on the right side of the church.

The preacher spoke a beautiful word before we sang Happy Birthday to both of his children as we crossed them over his body as his family tradition.

It was so beautiful, and I felt Junya's happiness from everyone being there and both his children celebrating their birthdays together just like he wanted. We were all given a red rose that we were to place on his casket. I let everyone go first because my vision was of me standing at his casket alone giving him my shoes and lifting him up and placing my hand over his casket. After everyone placed their roses on the casket the preacher, his mother, our sister, and other family members went back into the church for a dinner that was being provided. I stayed behind with Junya and walked to the casket just like in my vision. I placed my shoes in front of the casket and made jokes with Junya as if no one were there except me and him. I told him he could have those uncomfortable shoes he picked out for me that he loved so much. Everyone was laughing and not crying anymore. I felt peace all around me. I told him how much I love him and raised my hands just like God told me to do. It was as if I was lifting his spirit up, then I placed them over the casket faced down to what seemed like I was taking his spirit with me. I knew I was almost done with my vision. I walked away and started talking to his children's mother.

When the guys announced that they were going to put him down in the ground I looked back with a sad look remembering that my shoes were inside his casket with him in my vision not outside of it. I asked Junya to make a way in my mind. Then a woman I knew from childhood walked up to me and asked me what was wrong. I guess she knew by my facial expression. I told her about my vision of my shoes being inside the casket with my brother, but I did not want to ask the guys making their jobs more difficult. I said, "God will make a way"! Out of nowhere she walked up to the guys picked up my shoes and asked them to put them inside. They did with no problem. I was in disbelief that she did that for me. I asked someone to take a picture for me so I would never forget that moment. His son mother walked up and took the photo for me. I smiled so hard thanking them both for what they have done. I thanked God for making a way for everything that was done and being my guide through everything. Everything was perfect just like Junya wanted. I thanked the guys for placing my shoes with my brother as they began to lower him into the ground. I knew after that my job was done and now Junya could rest.

    I met up with Kayhiem and my family in the dining room. I was so happy to see everyone happy and enjoying themselves. I felt the peace in the air and knew that was all Junya ever wanted. I noticed that I did not really take any photos like that, but I knew the memory would always be with me forever. I talked to a lot of people as we stood in line to get our food and when I sat down to eat my little cousin came running to me. She asked me to follow her outside because she needed to show me something in the sky. When I ran outside with her, she pointed at the sky. When I looked up, I saw an angel in the sky over my jeep, then she showed me a photo that she caught prior to me coming outside of what seemed like Junya's hands over my jeep. Shortly after, the clouds started to get dark fast then it began to rain. Everyone said their goodbyes and left.

We got to our grandmother's house and said our goodbyes before getting back on the road as well. We prayed for our safe travel and left to go back to New York.

Chapter 7: FORGIVE THOSE WHOM TRESSPASS AGAINST YOU!

While driving back to New York I let my aunt drive first. I was still in disbelief of the journey I had down south. When I looked on Facebook people were posting about me speaking at the celebration. They could not believe what happened down there as well. At that very moment I realized that God, Angels, and the Holy spirit was all inside and outside of me everywhere working through, and with me to fulfill my purpose. Everything constantly played back in my head over and over the entire ride. Me, my aunt, and Kayheim spoke about the experience and how everything God told me prior to arriving in South Carolina came to pass. I went to sleep for a couple of hours and when I woke up, I took over the driving for the rest of our travels. The next morning on February 10, 2020 at about 10 a.m. we returned home in New York. When I walked through the door, my spirit spoke. It said, "Prepare yourself. We all unpacked and went to sleep.

On February 11, 2020 I woke up and went into the kitchen for some coffee. I felt so much pain and anger arising. It was not my anger I felt though, it was like I could feel a lot of different people's anger and pain inside of me from them. Then I felt that I must get on live and forgive the murderers so everyone could see and hear me. I was confused, so I asked, "Why God do you want me to forgive the people that murder my brother?" God told me I was forgiven for all the bad things I have done, and I am still a child of God. Same for the murderers, so I must forgive them and bring peace, because they are still his children too. Then I remembered what God showed me at the murder scene and how he tried to stop them from the murder prior to the incident, but their envy, jealousy, and anger built up a lot over time causing them to carry on with the murder. God showed me how Junya's soul was saved prior to him taking his last breath. I found my phone and my mother called me while I was cleaning. She told me that the murderers were on the run from the police because of what they done. They have not been caught or not turned themselves into authority.

The guy that murdered my brother name is Javon Hair and the other guy that drove Javon to kill Junya name is Dyshan Frasier. When my mother told me, they have not been found I got angry and started to cry. I heard in my right ear to pray. So, I began to pray, and the pain disappeared. I continued to listen to my mother repeat the story about what she found that really happened to Junya. It was the same story that I told her Junya showed me when I went to the crime scene. I thanked her for calling me and told her I love her as I hung up the phone.

I continued to clean the house with Kayheim until we were done, and my phone was charged. Then I felt like a power force inside my soul wanted me to speak to the people and forgive the murderers, so they could be brought to justice untouched to serve their time. When I got on live and wrote the title a lot of people started to join me as I spoke. I told them the message I received from God to forgive. I explained to them why God told me I had to forgive them. Then I asked the people to please let go of their anger and envy because that is what caused this murder in the first place. I told the people to please put down their guns and pray. Build a relationship with God and surrender to be led to greatness not destruction. Then I prayed with the people and ended the conversation telling them to let love guide them not hate. Anyone that watched the video was moved by it. I was moved by it. I could not even believe what I was saying and how God push it out my mouth to speak. It was amazing, touching, and unbelievable. After the video, I felt a sense of relief and a huge weight lifted of my shoulder. The same way I felt leaving South Carolina. A lot of people commented that God spoke through me to them. They liked and shared my video and it received almost 2,000 views. It was amazing and I was happy that people were able to find some peace in the death of Junya.

On February 13, 2020 I woke up to a lot of my family and childhood friends arguing and beefing back and forth on Facebook with one another. I saw how I was in the middle of all of it and did not comment on anything. God told me I had the power to speak to the people to bring peace and unity. I was afraid a little, but I knew God would help me in any assignment that was given to me, so I opened my mouth and I spoke on live. I told the people what I was witnessing from the people I love. I told them to activate the God inside of them for love and to be guided out of this misery and destruction. I called it God-Fi. I told them that I saw that they were being used just like those guys who murdered someone we all love and if they did not stop things would get worst. I gave them examples on how to activate God inside of them. I said we must humble ourselves so God can speak to us and we can hear the voice. We cannot hear or pay attention when anger, frustration, envy, or jealousy is involved. I told them we are all connected through God-fi, so we needed one another. I came up with a challenge to see who were the big people that would apologize to someone they hurt and tag them into the post. I ended the live by starting with myself and apologizing to everyone that I may have hurt in the past. Then I told them I love them all, they were beautiful people, and God loves them very much. People started to like and share that video as well. I got off Facebook because I felt that weigh lift off my shoulders again.

February 14, 2020 was an incredibly special day. It was Valentine's Day, Junya's daughter 1st birthday, and my preacher birthday. Me and my aunt got together and went live on Facebook to sing Happy birthday to them both. It was beautiful because my aunt has a voice of an angel. Then after, I noticed people were taking the challenge seriously and apologizing to one another sincerely. They used the hashtag #GOD_FI and tagged me in the post. As I scrolled up my timeline all I saw was love everywhere. I was so happy and so proud. My family and childhood friends were all finally bringing peace to their situations. It was an amazing day for me. Kayheim went out and surprised me with my favorite food and balloons. My two oldest daughters wrote me the best letters. I had everything I needed to enjoy my Valentine's Day. I was happy and I was blessed. I thanked God and my brother for everything.

On March 2, 2020 we were all introduced to the Coronavirus also known as COVID-19. This virus was extremely deadly, and the world was on lock down. No schools were opened, most businesses had to be shut down, everyone had to stay in their houses until told otherwise in most states. While New York was on locked down, I finished my second book that I was working on called, <u>Finding Mrs. Woodward</u>. I published it on Amazon on March 12, 2020. I am extremely happy about the publication of that book because it was an extension of my first book that I published called, <u>Is That You Mrs. Woodward.</u> I published that book on December 29, 2019. <u>Is That You Mrs. Woodward</u> spoke about a health teacher that helped me when I was fourteen years old. I wrote the book in hope of finding her again after sixteen years through faith.

Nine days after the publication she was found for me. I got to speak with her and catch up with her and my middle school, that helped me find her. I left an amazing memory with the school through my story and Mrs. Woodward left an amazing memory with me through our story. I was supposed to meet with Mrs. Woodward the day after my brother got shot, but never did. Before I found out about my brother, I was in the process of writing, <u>Finding Mrs. Woodward.</u> I put it on pause to be there for my brother and when I returned, I finished it and published it on March 12, 2020. I was enormously proud of myself for pushing through to complete the project that I never imagined would be.

Two days later March 14, 2020 I woke up and saw on Facebook that they found the two guys that murdered my brother. I was so happy dropping to my knees thanking God for doing what was promised to me. They were untouched and now could serve their time in prison for what they did to Junya. I got on Facebook live extremely happy and relieved to tell everyone that God delivered like I knew he would. I cried with the people and prayed with them. I told everyone to celebrate that day for our brother. Then it hit me, that when Junya came to see me in New York a couple of months prior, I told him a vision that God showed me about three books that I was going to write. I was to write a black book, a gold book, and a platinum book. I told him that, "**Is That You, Mrs. Woodward**" was my black book and the gold book would be about a CD that led me back to God. I told him that whatever God was cooking up I could not see all the details, but I knew my gold book would be amazing and mean a lot to me.

At that moment, I realized that my gold book was never about the CD itself. It was about my brother. His favorite color was gold. His clothing line that carried his brand was gold. He loved Gold! I could not believe what I saw. The CD by Jason Breland that I thought the book would be about is what helped me remain calm through Junya's entire situation to hear the God speak to me. It was so amazing to realize this. God finding Mrs. Woodward for me to write the second part was just a blessing in disguise to keep my faith and hold me off from writing my book until I realized it was about Junya the entire time. What an amazing God! After that, I continued to deliver the messages that God gave me and promote my books.

Chapter 8: What If?

On April 5, 2020 I realized that my menstrual period was late. So, I went into the bathroom with a pregnancy test to take it. Not thinking for a second that I would be pregnant after just having a baby girl six months before in October. When I looked at the test and it read positive, I was shocked. So many thoughts played in my head over and over. I thought about telling Kayheim. I thought about what others would say about me. I thought of how I would be able to care for another child after having three kids already. I thought about what my family would say. So many thoughts flew through my head and I just sat there for a while reflecting on all the negative thoughts and then I asked God, why is this happening now? Why now?

I sat there waiting for an answer still allowing the thoughts to float through my head. Then I heard Junya's voice asking me, what if it was a boy I was carrying? Then all the negative thoughts I was thinking altered. I asked myself that if I knew I was carrying the boy I always wanted would I still be thinking the way I was thinking. At that moment I needed time to reflect on the answer to that question. I said to myself if I were having my first son, I would not care what people would say. I would not care what my family would say. I would not care about how many children I already have. I would be happy. Then my spirit shifted. Truth is I would not care if it were a girl because all I cared about was a healthy child, but the fact of having my first son lingered in my mind heavily. So instead of taking the fears with me at that point I chose to take only the positive and get ready to hear about the negatives later.

Kayheim was not in the house at that moment, so I sent him a picture text of the pregnancy test because I could not wait until he got home. I wanted to hear how he felt about me being pregnant again. He felt exactly the way I pictured he would feel. He was extremely excited, and it helped me calm down a lot as well. He told me that no matter what we would stick together through everything and all would be well. If I knew I had God I was so relieved and able to continue my day without it affecting me too much. I knew I was about five weeks pregnant from my last menstrual period, so I told him that as well. Then I told him that I heard Junya's voice asking me how I would feel about having a boy. We reflected on that for a moment and we both got extremely happy. We knew the odds was slim because I had three girls already and he had one daughter outside of the three girls that I had. We continue to reflect on having a boy though. Then I realized that it was one month exactly from the day that Junya left us. We both reflect on that too. We ended our conversation with saying we love each other and no matter what everything would be okay.

About a week later the Coronavirus pandemic was rising and then the entire world was on lock down. Everything was getting crazy and scary. I was afraid for my children, family, and our lives. I played Jason Breland music a lot more than before and other gospel

CD to keep me calm and my family also. I remember one day when I was six weeks pregnant, I was in the kitchen listening to Jason Breland on some huge headphones washing dishes, and everything zoned out. Then I zoned into myself just like at Junya's celebration and received so many messages. It was from my ancestors and divine angels. They introduced themselves as such. They all told me how proud of me they were for what I have done for Junya and listening to their instruction to carry out the assignment that was needed of me. They told me how beautiful I am and how strong I am. They told me they had a gift for me. I asked what it was, and they said my gift was a boy and I was to name him Wisdom. I could not believe what I was hearing and feeling. It felt like a vibration of pure love. I just stayed there zoned in crying and thanking them. Communicating with them was of nothing I have ever seen or felt before. I felt so loved, so free, so happy, and so light as if I could fly.

I could feel my second daughter tapping me asking if I were okay, but I would not let go of the communication with them to answer her. As I stood there numb, I lift my hands in the air thanking them for the gift that they have given me. Then it was like a force pushing my hands down near my side and I asked what that meant, and I heard meditation. They told me a lot of times that they love me, and they would continue to guide me and watch over me. I kept crying and thanking them as everything faded away. I began singing loudly crying and praising God. I could not believe it. If you would have told me that a year prior, I would not have believed you. My daughter kept asking me if I was okay and this time, I turned to her and dropped down to her level and hugged her so tight as I told her I was better than I have ever been. I explained to Kayheim about what I saw and heard. I told him about our gift that was given to me. He did not look surprised because he was always guiding me to get to where I was. I realized how everything really is connected and if we are not paying attention or fight it, we could miss it. At that time, I kept all the information to myself other than telling Kayheim and the children. I did not announce the pregnancy or what I have been told. Partly because I felt no one would believe me.

When I was about three months pregnant, I got another visit from my divine angels and ancestors. I was in the car with Kayheim and the children listening to Jason Breland music and 90's love music. While I was driving and listening to the music, I zoned out again and began to zone within myself just like before. I knew what was happening, but I did not know why this time. Then I heard angels speaking to me asking me if I remember them. I stood quiet on the outside but answered them within and said yes. They told me they were there to give me another gift. I asked what it was after saying hello. They told me they were not just giving me the gift of a little boy, but the little boy would carry the soul of my brother Junya. I was so shocked and confused on how that could be, or if that were even possible. I just listened and cried as I received the information because no matter what I believed before, I knew that they never misguided me the entire time. I asked, "how and why"? They told me I was being given the soul of Junya as a Prophecy inside my baby because of what I did for him and listening and obeying their instructions. They also told me because of Junya trying to bring peace prior to him leaving. It was unbelievable to hear such things. They thanked me and I thanked them.

After I received the message I zoned back to driving. The entire time I was driving and could see and focus, but also receive the message at the same time. Trust and faith were there, and it was at a high frequency. I could not hold the tears back. They were falling so fast and Kayhiem who was in the passenger side asked me what was wrong with me. I told him what just happened and what I heard. He was in amazed, but again did not look surprised. I pulled up to our house and told him to take the children inside because I needed a minute to reflect on what just happened. When they exit the car, I found parking and shut the car off. Holding my mouth, I started crying harder than ever before. Yelling out Junya name and thanking the universe at the same time. Thinking over and over what I just heard. So many thoughts ran through my head. I felt so unworthy of the gift, yet I was being trusted and chosen for it. I stood there for about twenty minutes allowing the message to play over and over. Then I dried my tears and went inside the house.

When I got inside Kayhiem already had the children in bed and I sat at the computer and started researching the prophecy I received to try to understand what was happening and if it was even possible. I started with reincarnation. I read so many stories and did so much research I became obsessed with it. I stop speaking on live as much as I used to. I even deactivated my Facebook page for a while so I could focus only on my family and the gift I was given. I learned that reincarnation was true, and many studies have proven that. I learned that what I once thought about death was not the truth. I used to think that when we died that was it. We go to heaven or hell and stay there for eternity and never come back.

When I started my research, I never believed that again. A lot of information that I researched led me to other answers that I needed to be answered and that is when I knew my angels, was leading me right through the information. My spirit would confirm it when I saw certain information, I would get so many goosebumps on my arms, shivers through my body, and so emotional. I learned that when we pass on to the spirit world our soul chooses to leave our physical bodies. After our soul leaves our physical body, we go back into the spirit world. Sometimes we stay there for a long time and hang out in the spirit world and sometimes we want to return to the physical world immediately to either finish things we felt we left uncompleted before, or simply to help people.

A lot of times when we reincarnate, we may come back through the same bloodline as before as someone else. Our soul would linger around someone that is about to conceive and at the point of conception choose its parents. That is when I learned that we choose our parents, as a soul. The soul would then check back and forth with the baby that is growing within the mother's stomach while pregnant to make sure they still want to come back in the physical world. That is when I learned that a lot of times when woman have a miscarriage for no proven reason the soul may decide not to want to come back in the physical world just yet. So, the soul checks out with the baby and the woman may lose the baby. We as the physical beings try to find physical ways to understand the reason why the baby was lost through technology and doctors, but the story is more than we could understand.

If the soul chooses to stay with the baby, then during the entire nine months the soul would continue to check in with the physical baby growing during pregnancy. At the point of birth is when the soul and the physical baby connects with one another for life in the physical world. Many studies and stories have proven this fact from children at young ages remembering who they were in their past lives. They may point to a photo and say their name that they remembered before or they may have certain gifts at a young age that they remembered from their past lives that have not ever been taught to them in this life.

Some children may have birth marks from their previous life as well. Some children may be terrified of something that never hurt them in this life that may have killed them in their past life. I read a story about an elderly man that was about to die, and he gave his son a specific gold watch with his name imprinted on the inside. The son told his father that he would miss him, and he loved him very much. The father told him he would be back in another life eventually. Then two years later the son and his wife got pregnant and had a son. When the baby was two years old, he went into his parents' room and saw the watch on the dresser. He pointed at the watch and called out the name of his grandfather. The son was amazed because he never told his baby the name of his grandfather. When the son picked up the watch and handed it to his baby, he flipped the watch inside out and pointed at the name and said his grandfather name again. That is when the son knew that his baby boy came back as his grandfather. I read many other stories as well, but for some reason this one stuck with me and I wanted to share it with you guys.

My research continued and I learned so much. I learned enough to believe, even though I believed when I heard it from my divine angel, but the information I learned helps me communicate what I saw and heard to my readers. I thank God for leading me to the information to be able to express myself through my writing. At this point, I still did not tell anyone other than Kayhiem and the children, because I did not know where to start and I did not want anyone telling me different from their beliefs. I knew that if someone told me a year ago about this, then I would not believe them. Things change when you go through them. My gift is to write, so I realized that writing a book on my brother would be the best way to explain what happened to me this year and my experiences as a connection.

At this time, I have not received any test to

prove that the sex of my baby was a boy, but that did not stop me from knowing. I gave away all my baby girl clothes as she grew, because I knew we were buying boy clothes for our son. I started to tell a selected four individuals about the prophecy instead of everyone. The people that I told said they believed me, but also asked me what if I was wrong. When those words were spoken to me it felt like a sign of disrespect.

The reason for that is because I told them it was from God and I felt like if we believed in God, then how could it be doubted. I did not take it personal though, because once again I said I believe in God, but if someone told me what I am telling you a year ago I probably would not believe it either. Three out of the selected four, asked me if it would be a girl, then what would I do or say then. I told them that the prophecy was real, and it would be a boy, so I did not have to think about what if. I told them that the truth would soon come to pass just like everything else. My faith was extremely high in God. That is when I realized that even though we may believe and follow God, we can be turned away so quickly by the things of this world. We must continue to believe in the voice of God within us, even if we cannot see or understand now. What a lesson!

The Coronavirus pandemic was rising fast making everything change the way the world used to work. This virus was a blessing in disguise for me because instead of waiting until I was about 20 weeks (5 months) pregnant to get the result of the sex of my baby through an ultrasound, I was able to receive bloodwork at 16 weeks (4 months) pregnant. I was so happy because I was impatient. I wanted to prove to the selected few that I was having a boy and prove to myself that I was not crazy for what I heard. The lady that took my blood told me that I had to wait 4 days to receive my results. During the wait, the selected few tried to change my mind and it seemed intense to me. When the fourth day came, I did not receive no phone calls from the doctor's office, and I became even more impatient. On the fifth day I started calling the doctor's office every day for two weeks straight. Then a doctor told me the test took two weeks and they would call me when they got the results. I was so anxious inside to find out.

My youngest daughter had an appointment with the doctor in the same doctor's office a couple days later, so I told Kayhiem I would go upstairs to my doctor then, because the results should be in by that day. I did not call anymore I just waited till the appointment. The night before my youngest daughter's appointment, Kayhiem and I was talking about finding out the baby's sex. We tried so many known traditions to figure out the sex of the baby and they all pointed to the baby being a girl.

That night Kayhiem asked me a question that I never thought would never come from him. He said, "Baby! What if it's a girl"! I looked at him in disbelief of what he was saying and asked him why he would say that. He said that he was just looking at the bigger picture and wanted to prepare us just in case we were having another girl. I told him I knew it was a boy, but he still asked me what if. I was not prepared to answer that question and for a second I let it sink into my mind and

I said, "If the baby is a girl, I would love her just like the rest!" The entire night that question played in my mind and I spoke to God saying I believe you. I trust in you.

The next morning at the doctor office with my youngest daughter I got so impatient waiting on her doctor to arrive. So, I told Kayhiem to stay with her and I went upstairs to my doctor for the results. After I told the receptionist my name and why I was there she told me to have a seat and the doctor would be right with me. I was so anxious that I could feel my hands sweating while I waited. It felt like forever for her to call my name, but it was only 6 minutes after watching my clock. When she called me into the room and sat me down, she asked me what sex of the baby I wanted to have. Even though I wanted a boy, I told her a girl because I was preparing myself for that answer.

She apologized to me and said, "I'm sorry Ms. Garland it's a boy"! I jumped up and stood in shock. I asked her again what she said, and she said, "It's a boy!" I asked her if she was playing with me and she said no. She then showed me the paperwork with the sex of the baby circled. I gave her a huge hug thanking her. I started yelling thanking God. I was sweating holding my head still yelling. I said, "God did it"! I asked her for the paperwork to show Kayhiem. She asked me why I was so happy when I wanted a girl. I told her I was just preparing myself for that answer, and I really wanted a boy because I already have three girls. The doctor instantly got happy with me and I thanked her. I thought about Kayhiem and ran out the office to go tell him.

When I got to the elevator, I began pressing the button to what seemed like one hundred times until it finally came. It felt like the ride was so slow and could not get me downstairs fast enough. As I walked back to my daughter's doctor office, I began crying telling God thank you over and over. I told him he is the best and always keeps his promises. When I got closer to Kayhiem, I dried my face because I wanted to trick him. When I got in the room where they were being held at, I handed him the paper with the sex on it. While he looked for the answer, I asked him what he thought the answer was. He looked at my face and said it was a girl. I shook my head no and pointed at the sex of the baby on the paper. His eyes lit up in amazement. I told him God did what he said. Then I broke down while he stared at the results, but this time I could not breathe and started to gag. Kayhiem tried to calm me down and I told him that I had to get outside because I was about to faint, and I could not breathe.

We ran outside together. I took deep breaths to gasp the air. We both were in disbelief. I was relieved that there would be no more "what ifs"! As we walked to the car, I called the selected few and told them the results. Then I called my mother and told her. She could not believe it either. Then I just chatted with Kayhiem on how he felt, and how I felt. When we were about to enter the car, a pigeon poop, and it dropped on Kayhiem's shirt. We started laughing. I told him that everyone says that's good luck. It was amazing. We were sharing this experience together. I was staring at his smile and was even more happy of how happy he was. I just wanted to see what else the prophecy would bring. I asked the universe and my angels to guide me and I would listen to everything and not allow no one to get in the way of the prophecy. Later that day, Kayheim and I decided to post the great news on Facebook so our family and friends could see it. So, I reactivated my Facebook and posted, "It's a boy" with our due date.

Chapter 9: Wisdom Junya Prophecy

    Normally, when I thought of someone who received a prophecy, I pictured it being all peaches and cream, but it was not until I received one that I saw things differently sometimes. When I first received the gift, it was the most beautiful thing ever. I knew some people would doubt what I saw and heard, so that part would be a challenge, but it started to become a little more difficult than that. After Kayhiem and I found out the sex of our baby arguments between us started. First, we had an argument about the name of the baby. Kayhiem said that I wanted to name our baby's entire name after I found out the sex of him. It was the truth, because after we found out that it was a boy, I told him that Wisdom Junya Prophecy would be an amazing name for him. The name just came to me out of nowhere. I knew once I found out it was the soul of Junya, I would want his name to be in there somewhere. He felt as if I took the baby entire name and named him what I wanted. I felt like it was only right, that the name stood as is because we both understood the prophecy and he never wanted his first son to be named after him anyway. It was a petty argument, but that was just the beginning to my problems.

    Shortly after, we found out that my grandfather was on life support, so we needed to travel to South Carolina immediately. Kayhiem decided not to go with me this time. I guess he was tired of all the deaths. People have been dying a lot during the Coronavirus which was also taking a toll on us. Right after losing my brother Kayhiem lost his uncle due to the Coronavirus. That hit his family hard and we had to be the one to break the news to his grandmother about her only son, so I understood why he passed on my grandfather funeral. I wanted to go down south to support my family but did not want to go to any funerals while I was pregnant and super emotional. During the visit down south, I felt all the emotions Junya was trying to tell me about when he visited me. Emotions, depression, and paranoia covered me while I was there. I just wanted to go home the entire time. Me and my family fell out with each other during the trip as well.

When I got back home, I knew I had to heal from everything that went on down there. I remember sitting on the couch the next day after I arrived and asked God why did I feel the way I did in South Carolina? Then I heard Junya's voice telling me it was because I took him back down there. At that moment, I realized that all the things that Junya was trying to get me to understand that he was feeling I felt. He had falling out with some of his family members, he felt paranoid of his enemies and police, and he was extremely depressed that no one was seeing what he saw. That healing process took a toll on me and my pregnancy. It took me a while to recover. I did not want to write or anything. I caught myself falling into a deep depression.

Every day was a struggle to get up from where I was. It was so dark. I missed my brother so much. I was not talking to my sisters. I found myself crying a lot and I just wanted it all to stop. I felt like I had no one to talk to except God and one of my aunts that lives in Texas. Her name is Angela, but we all called her Angel. She was one of the selected four I told you about earlier. She helped me a lot to get out of the depression by talking to me. She also would send me things to watch so I could pick myself up and not give up. She would always be there for me when I needed her. When I wrote my first book, she stayed on the phone with me for hours while I read the entire book to her. She helped me a lot then and now. She helped me understand my feelings and how not to run from them but to embrace them. She would stay on the phone with me for hours allowing me to vent and then giving me positive energy and positive feedback. It helped a lot, but something was still missing.

When I was alone, I would still cry and ask God how I get up. I would ask God to help me move forward. Then one day I asked Junya how he continued his journey with all these feelings following him. I remember laying in the bed as tears fell down my eyes and me holding my stomach because it was so tight. I felt like I needed to see Junya, so I went to his Facebook page. At first, I got sad by looking at his beautiful face and thinking I would never see him again then I scrolled down to his videos and even though he left a lot of them behind one specific one stood out to me. His face on the video looked like he was crying, so I clicked on it. What I saw next was the missing piece I needed to move forward. He started off telling us that he had just left an event with celebrities that all loved him and supported him. He felt amazing energy around them and knew that was where he belonged. He told us that even though a lot of people that knew him did not give him a chance or believed in him he would never be that way with them. As tears fell down his eyes, he said he wanted his dream so bad and he knew he would make it no matter what, because he would never stop.

That day I cried with my brother so much watching the video over and over until I said, "Brother, I promise I will never stop"! I thanked him so much for leaving that video. It takes a strong man to do what he did. I dried my tears and looked at a lot of photos of him smiling and then I heard him say, "Write sis"! I grabbed my pen and paper and began to write. My emotions poured unto my paper and released from my body. I felt so much better. I felt like I could continue this journey. I listened to as much inspirational speeches as I could to keep striving for greatness. I knew that if I gave up no one would hear my story. I knew that my story would help others just like his story helped me. After outlining my book, I knew I had to forgive myself and others to be free of anything holding me back. So, I started with my youngest sister Rella. I reached out to her on the phone and we spoke for three hours straight. We spoke the entire time about Junya. It felt so amazing to be able to speak about Junya for a long time and get all our feelings that we felt inside, out. She also said the same thing. She felt that even though she spoke to other people about him it felt like because they did know him, they could not really understand her feelings. I did understand. I understood exactly how she felt.

I told her about the book I was writing and the gift of the prophecy I received. I told her the name of the baby and she loved it. We spoke about still speaking with Junya throughout my experience. She told me at first, she thought she was crazy and told me about different experiences when she just knew Junya was there guiding her. I told her she was not crazy at all and I was experiencing the same things. I told her what Junya said about how I felt when we went to South Carolina. She told me that she believed me and told me stories that they spoke about daily and the feelings he was feelings. She told me some of his experiences that I did not even know about that he told her. I understood why he did not tell me though. I probably would have been even harder on him. By the time our conversation ended I felt so much better. I was happy that I spoke to my sister and was able to speak about my brother with no judgement, just pure love, and respect. She asked me to be the God mother of my baby, and I agreed. I felt that it was only right knowing she loved Junya just as much as me.

 A couple of days later my spirit guided me to speak with my mother. I was so emotional. I was breaking down as if it finally hit me that my brother was gone. I did not understand why I started feeling that way with the knowledge I knew. So, I called my mother. When I got on the phone with her, I apologized for the way I was when we traveled down south. She gave me some motherly advice and then I broke down. I told her my brother was really gone. She said she knew eventually I would break down because I was too calm the entire time. I told her about my book and how I had to revisit every memory and it was breaking me down, but Junya would not let me sleep without finishing what I started. She told me it was okay to feel the way I felt. I was happy to speak with my mother, it really helped me emotionally to continue the journey I was on.

As I continue to write and revisit every memory and emotion of this year 2020, I still break down numerous of times, but each time God and Junya picked me up. His videos continue to guide me to the next step and help me realize why I was experiencing the feelings I was feeling. One day when I was writing about the day of the shooting I broke down and I went to Facebook and typed in Junya's name. All my photos and his photos that he commented on popped up.

Then I saw one photo of my first book that he posted, and I commented on telling him, "Bro!!! You know how much I love you! I thank God for the man, father, and brother you are. Keep doing what you are doing because I believe in you always. Even though you are my younger brother you have shown me bigger visions for life and my purpose on Earth. I love you so very much. Thank you for all the love and support you have always given me." That comment that I wrote under his post made me smile, because I knew I always made sure he knew how I felt about him. Then I realized that he commented back, and I never answered it. He said, "No problem big sis! I love you to death!" I broke down when I saw that. Thanking him for guiding me back to that post to know how much he love me and to know that he knew how much I loved him. That really helped me continue this book and get past the part I needed to complete. Being pregnant, emotional, and trying to write about Junya was so difficult.

I spoke to my mother again and told her the name of my baby. "Wisdom Junya Prophecy is what we named him," I told her. She said she did not like the name Wisdom, and I should name him knowledge. I felt hurt because I knew that name was told to me to give to the baby, but my mother did not know so I told her I would think about it. The next day when I was about to start writing I thought about what my mother had said and decided to look up wisdom and knowledge in the dictionary.

The definition of **Wisdom** is the quality of having experience, knowledge, and good judgement. The definition of **Knowledge** is facts, information, and skills acquired by a person through experience or education. Then I looked up wisdom vs. knowledge- **Wisdom** involves a healthy dose of perspective and the ability to make sound judgements about a subject while **Knowledge** is simply knowing through research. Then I realized that the angels named him Wisdom for a reason because I got the experience, knowledge, and good judgement from within. Knowledge means researching to learn something outside yourself. Then I decided to look up prophecy so I would know why that name stood out to me. Three definitions stood out to me, so I used them all to communicate to you guys. **Prophecy** is a prediction. **Prophecy** is a message claimed to have been communicated by God. **Proph-**

ecy is a revelation of divine will be concerning events to come. So, when I put his entire name together, I got the experience, knowledge, and good judgement from within (**Wisdom**) from Junya (**Junya**) by the message that was communicated to me by God (**Prophecy**). What an amazing God! What an amazing name! All the experiences that I have been going through this entire year and this entire pregnancy whether I felt it was good or bad was for a reason. Through time and writing I realized all the messages that normally our busy lives would hide from us.

For a couple of weeks, I stopped writing because I did not get the urge to. I got a little worried and began asking God why. I was not hearing any messages or anything. Then after a while I realized that I was trying to rush this book. In trying to rush it that is when I would get depressed or feel weird. That resulted in me not wanting to touch my work. Then something else would happen that added to the story. As I wrote it down, I noticed that this story was not to be rushed. I still had things I needed to go through to finish it.

When everything was a standstill for me fears and doubt would begin to rise, and I would feel like giving up or just feel impatient. No matter what, I refused to give up on my brother and my story, because it means so much to me and I could feel that it means so much to him. To past the time me, and my children would go through the baby clothes and I would picture me holding him and talking with him. That helped past the time along. Then, I started having visions and dreams about the baby and the prophecy seemed so much more real. It felt like I was in another world that I did not want to waked up from. I had many dreams of me holding Wisdom, but I could not see his face. I had a dream that after I pushed him out the doctor handed him to me, and I could feel his entire body. Also, the heat from his body against my body, but I still could not see his face. I did not want to let him go. I told him a million times that I loved him, and I would protect him. One dream I had helped me to realized that this book was not to be completed until I gave birth to him. In the dream I was giving birth and I heard soft music playing in the background. As I pushed each push there was a light that shined brighter each time. When he was out in the world, the light stood with him as he was given to me. When I saw him, I knew that my brother was here again. I still could not see his face, but I felt his spirit in the room and in my baby when I held him. When I woke up all those fears and doubts disappeared, and I grew more patience to wait it through and just continue to write about experiences that I experienced.

Chapter 10: Fear…False Evidence Appearing Real

One day when I went to the doctor, they told me that I had Gestational Diabetes due to carrying the baby, and I must use insulin for the remaining of my pregnancy. I knew that would happen because I had it with my prior pregnancy, so I was not shocked. When they gave me an ultrasound at 30 weeks, they found more fluid on one side of his brain than the other. I knew something was up, because two doctors rushed in my room and began measuring the same spots. When they explained it to me, tears filled my eyes and fear filled my heart, then I heard Junya's voice and he said, "I'm ok sis"! Then the tears dried without even falling. I told the nurse that I was not worried about it, because God is in control. She scheduled me another ultrasound at 34 weeks, because usually that is when the head of the baby would be turn down towards the uterus and they could run clearer test. So, I put it behind me until then.

The appointment went well. The fluid was the same amount not causing any panic, just something to watch after the baby was born. I continued to go to my weekly appointments to check on the baby. At, week 36, two weeks before I gave birth FEAR attacked me again. I mean fear has always try to come into my mind through everything that I experienced. Trying to make me stop my plans, but it was not until I started paying attention and becoming more conscious of what was happening, I could control it from affecting me. I spoke to my doctor and she said Wisdom was getting too big.

At week 39, he would be 10 lbs., and that was signs of a C-section. She considered that I have a C-section for Wisdom. I told her that I gave birth to a big baby before, and I would control the Gestational Diabetes that made him get bigger fast. She said it was my choice. We decided that the best method was for us to have was a scheduled induction to speed up the labor process. We scheduled the date for 11/18/2020 and twice a week appointment for us to watch Wisdom's brain, weight, and his movements. Gestational Diabetes pregnant woman have larger numbers of still born babies due to the infant's weight and that was the main problem that my doctors wanted to prevent.

As the days got closer FEAR kept sneaking in. It was always on my mind about the birth of Wisdom. Was he going to be okay? Am I eating the right things? Are my sugar numbers too high or low? Should I have a C-section? Why I have not I heard from Junya in a couple weeks? My family would not be able to visit me in the hospital like they usually do due to the Coronavirus. I got so fed up with thinking about it all and just wanted answers right away. I would go outside and ask the universe what was happening? Then, I would listen to motivational speakers such as, Steve Harvey, Denzel Washington, Ralph Smart, Steven Furtick, and Tyler Perry. After, I felt so much better. I kept moving toward my main vision. I still went through the normal pregnancy stuff like crying, rushing to get everything prepared for his arrival, and packing our bags.

The morning of November 18, 2020, Kayheim and I woke up and cleaned up the house. We took our showers and got dressed to start our day. In the mist of that we celebrated. We began dancing, telling each other how much we love one another, and congratulating each other while answering all the calls from our families wishing us well on our journey. Our induction was scheduled for 4 p.m. that evening, so we left out the house at around 11 a.m.

First, we went to go get our amazing Dunkin Donut's pumpkin spice coffee. Then, we went to pick up other supplies we would need for our stay at the hospital. I told him that I needed a small fan because the last time I gave birth to our daughter he stood and fanned me with his hands the entire time. So, having a small fan that he could just hold to my face would be much better for the both of us. Around 1 p.m. that evening we were so excited and wanted to be near the hospital, so we ended up parking near the hospital and eating lunch across the street.

We ate in the car, because of the Coronavirus we were not allowed to sit and eat in the restaurant. That did not stop us though. We had a great time in the car. Talking, laughing, listen to music, and listening to one another until the time came. At 3:32 p.m. we entered the building and walked to the receptionist. Kayhiem had to stay downstairs until I was registered and got my room for the induction. It took about 15 minutes with Albert Einstein hospital in Bronx, NY.

I got into my gown and they hooked me up to the

monitors to prepare for the procedure. Kayheim came inside the room shortly after and settled in. He looked so happy, and so ready. His energy helped me to remain calm during the entire process. The doctors and nursed came into our room to introduce themselves as the night crew.

Then, they began asking a million questions that was protocol for pregnancy and the Coronavirus. The nurses explained that we needed to get tested, which we knew prior to arriving at our appointment. They gave us many options, so we chose to be swabbed by our throats instead of our nostrils. After the test came back negative, the doctors began the first part of the induction around 8 p.m. that night. She checked my cervix and realized that I had dilated two centimeters, which was the beginning stages of labor. You must dilate 10 centimeters to be considered in active labor or time to push.

Before the medicine was started, my main doctor came inside the room to speak with us about the C-section once more. She went over the risks again with us. She said that a large baby could end up fracturing their shoulders during birth while trying to past through the birth canal. The shoulders also may get stuck in the birth canal causing the baby to lose oxygen. It was like she was trying to push me towards a C-section, but I just kept telling her that I wanted to have a vaginal birth. She became out of breath trying to persuade me to do the C-section. I asked her to calm down and told her everything would be fine with the baby if we proceed with the vaginal birth.

I knew what my dreams showed me and, in my dreams,, I was pushing him out. After she left the room, another lady came inside our room asking us how we felt so far and if we had any complaints. I felt that was the perfect time to tell her how I felt about so many people telling me I had a large baby and the all the risks I knew about prior to me coming there. I explained to the lady that I did not want anyone else coming to tell me about his weight or risks. I began to cry while I was saying this to her, because in my mind, heart, spirit, and soul I knew he was not 10 lbs. yet. I pushed out an 8lb. 12oz. baby before. Which I spoke about in my previous book, "Is That You Mrs. Woodward?"

I did not want anything else messing up the energy that I was trying to create for Wisdom or myself prior to his birth. Then, they began the first part of the induction. They put an IV in my arm to give me fluids and Pitocin to speed up the labor at around 10 p.m. They checked my cervix again and I dilated 4 centimeters. They asked me if I wanted an Epidural injection for pain. I told them I did. After I received the Epidural injection, I was told to relax and rest while the Pitocin worked its magic.

Kayheim went to sleep before me. I felt extremely restless thinking about everything that happened this year, also meeting our son for the first time. I began talking to God saying how I felt about everything I have been through and telling him I trust him. After getting everything off my mind, I was able to go to sleep. About 8 a.m. on November 19, 2020 all the doctors and nurses began to change shifts. The new doctors and nurses came into my room to introduce themselves and put their names on my board, so I could remember. We all knew that we were going to deliver Wisdom that day. My doctor checked me to see if I dilated any more than the 4 centimeters before. When she checked me, I dilated 6 centimeters around 8:30 a.m. They decided it was time to break my water to speed up the process. Once my water was broken, she told me that it would not be long before the baby came. She told me to call her if I felt a lot of pressure in my back.

Once she left the room, Kayheim and I looked at each other with huge smiles on our faces. Kayheim said we should try to get more rest before Wisdom's arrival. Then he turned over on his chair and fell out. My nurse came inside the room and gave me a huge ball with a flat space in the middle to rest my legs while they stayed opened for the baby to come down. She asked me if I needed anything before leaving the room. When she left the room, it was peaceful and quiet, making it the perfect time to mediate and talk to God. Instead of me talking, I just laid there and allowed all my thoughts to past through my mind.

I began thinking about my dreams of me pushing him out and the doctors handing him to me. Then I thought about why I have not heard from Junya in a couple of weeks. As all these thoughts started rushing in, I started to feel light as if I were floating. I felt this sense of calmness over my body. I felt like I was rising from the bed and floating through the room. Everything began to move in a slow motion. An enormous love vibration enter my spirit and I heard Junya's voice again finally. He said, "I'm ready sis!" I said, "Bro, what do you mean you are ready?" Then he said, "Call the doctor, I'm ready sis!" I felt a huge amount of pressure down my back after that, so at that moment I knew I dilated 10 centimeters and it was time to deliver the baby.

I pressed the button for the doctor to come and when she entered the room, I told her I dilated 10 centimeters. She told me that I did not know, and she had to check my cervix. When she checked my cervix she said, "How does fully dilated sound!" I said, "Okay." I did not seem as surprised as she thought, because I already had confirmation from my Junya. Kayheim stood up next to me as the nurses began to break down my bed to prepare me to push. One of the nurses took the big ball from me, but they were taking too long to prepare the bed and I could feel the baby coming down, so I told Kayheim to give me the ball back so my legs could stay opened and relaxed. He plugged up the small fan and my phone rung. It was my oldest sister and she wanted to stay on the phone with me while I gave birth, so I had Kayheim put the phone on speaker and place it at the top of his chair so she could hear the whole thing.

As the doctors prepare, Kayheim rubbed my forehead asking me if I was okay and I said I was fine. I was still in meditation watching everything around me eager to see my dream come to light. The room was still moving in slow motion and I was breathing in and out in slow motion with it. When everything was prepared, so they removed the ball and placed both of my feet on the feet holders at the bottom of the bed for support. It was finally time to push. The nurse that stood to the left of me, her name is Laura and she told me that when I push, she would help push my left leg to my chest and Kayheim was to do the same with my right side. Another nurse was standing in front of me and she was going to count to ten during each contraction for me to hold the push in place. None of the doctors were in the room with me, because three other women were having their babies at the same time and they thought because Wisdom was so big, that I would take the most time. Laura told us that instead of waiting for the doctors we were going to practice. We were okay with that because our prior pregnancy took two hours to push the baby out, so practice was a great idea.

I felt a contraction and Laura saw the contraction on the screen monitor. She told me to place my hands behind my legs pulling them towards me, take a deep breathe and hold it, then push and hold it until the count of ten. The first push was hard because I felt like I could not hold my breath that long, but when I blew off at the count of five, she said it was okay we were practicing. She told me to relax and wait for another contraction. Laura said that we were going to do three sets of counting to ten and holding my breath through each contraction. I began getting anxious as if I were getting anxiety. My palms began to sweat, and my face began to sweat, as I thought to myself that I would not be able to do it.

FEAR sneaked in again, but this time I breathed hard in and out as the thought past my mind. Then my entire body calmed down and I felt the vibration of the room.

I felt the energy of everything around me. The more I breathed, the more I felt like I could control everything that was happening. Kayheim grabbed the fan and asked me if I wanted him to wipe my sweat off my forehead and I turned my head slowly looking at him, calm and said no. Another contraction was coming, and my nurse asked me if I was ready to push. I looked at her calm, and said, "Yes". I placed my hands behind my legs, pulled them close, took a deep breathe, and held my breathe for ten seconds as I pushed. This time I was able to hold it the entire time. I did it two more times back-to-back.

When I realized that if I remained calm and listen to the voices around me, I was in control of Wisdom entering the world. So, I zoned into myself and let all three of their voices vibrate through my ears and into my spirit. Laura said, "You are doing great!" I let that echo in my ears as I silently repeated what she said in my head three times. Then I heard Kayheim said, "Baby, you can do this! You are a champ!" I repeat that three times in my head silently. Then the nurse in front of me started counting as I began to push again, and I told that her to please keep counting as her voice vibrated in my head calming me. Using them all as my head coaches and keeping myself calm gave me a strength I did not know I had. Through each push I thought about what everyone said about him and used it as motivation to push harder and hold my breathe longer.

I started pushing at 10:18 a.m. After the third set of pushes his head popped out! I could not believe it. The nurses did not believe it. Kayheim could not believe it. The nurses told me to hold my next push while they grab the doctors. The doctors came rushing in telling me to not push. I told them to hurry because the baby wanted to come out. It seemed like forever for them to get it together and for a minute I was getting upset, but I remember my breathing and calmed down. I turned to Kayheim and continue to breath slowly. I felt like I was squishing his head, so I keep my legs opened and tried not to put any pressure on his head remembering the extra fluid he had.

Then the doctors told me they were ready, and I grabbed my legs, held my breath, and push hard. He popped out and everyone was yelling with excitement. It was 10:28 a.m. making it only 20 minutes for him to come out into the world. Wisdom let out a huge cry and I was so happy. They put Wisdom in my arms just like the dream and the light shown around him. When I took him, he was warm and perfect. When I looked at him, I began to cry. All the doubt, all the fears, and all the thoughts stopped. I told him I loved him so much and thanked him for choosing me. I looked at Kayheim and he was so happy and he kissed me and told me I did it. I did the impossible. I proved all the doctors wrong. I kept my faith in God and listened each step of the way.

He was 9 lbs. 2.oz. of perfection. I immediately noticed that he had twelve fingers just like Kayheim did when he was born. I showed Kayheim and his smile grew larger. He could not believe it. I heard my sister yelling in the background saying I did so great and she was proud of me. The doctors couldn't believe what was happening. They were preparing for a big baby that may fracture his shoulders, but everything went perfect. I had no stitches needed, he was extremely healthy, and I was in no pain. I held him so tight not wanting to let him go. About forty minutes after birth Wisdom opened his eyes. I began to cry again because I knew it was the soul of my brother. I could see it in his eyes. I could feel it holding him. Everything seemed like a dream, but it was not, it was real. I was really experiencing everything. Holding Wisdom near my heart as we shared skin-to-skin was the only thing that showed me it was all real. I felt at peace, I felt free, I felt loved. As the nurses wheeled us in the wheelchair to our main room for the remaining of our stay, all the doctors and other nurses started clapping. They told me I did a great job. They said my birth was the fast and calmed compared to the other woman. They looked so shocked. I just thanked them while holding and looking my son, because that is all that mattered to me. I knew that this seemed like a regular birth of a child to the doctors, but I knew the gift that was given to me behind the scenes. That is what made things more special.

Now, I do not know what the Prophecy will bring in the future, but I have a vision that the soul of Junya that lives in Wisdom will bring great things to Earth. I believe that whatever Junya had planned for his life, he was not done and through Wisdom he would be able to finish it. I also have a vision that this book would have many parts to it as Wisdom grows. I pray that this story touches my readers, as it has touched my heart and healed me from the lost of my brother. This story has taught me that our connection to one another is bigger than we could ever imagine. Allowing God to guide us through each connection with one another is the key to life. Having patience, forgiveness, and faith will help us surrender everything to the Universe for our greater good. Thank all you for experiencing this part of my life with me. I love you all!!!!

Made in the USA
Middletown, DE
30 May 2023

31189625R10070